My Daily
Psalms & Prayers

Publications International, Ltd.

Christine A. Dallman is a freelance writer living near Everett, Washington. She is the author of *Daily Devotions for Seniors,* an inspirational resource for maturing adults, as well as co-author of several other PIL titles.

Randy Petersen is a writer and church educator from New Jersey with more than 40 books to his credit, including *Daily Dose of Knowledge: Bible, God's Answers to Tough Questions,* and *Why Me, God?*

Cover art: iStockphoto; Photodisc

Art Explosion; Brand X Pictures; iStockphoto; Jupiter Images; Photodisc; PIL Collection; Shutterstock

ISBN-13: 978-1-4508-0407-3
ISBN-10: 1-4508-0407-1

Manufactured in China.

8 7 6 5 4 3 2 1

Library of Congress Control Number: 2010927711

Timeless Psalms and Prayers

or many believers, the Book of Psalms is a favorite Old Testament book because its verses express much of what they feel regarding their relationship with God. Each psalm was written to be set to music for worship. Psalms, a collection of 150 poems, was literally ancient Israel's hymnal. Today, it remains a source of inspiration, comfort, and encouragement as a prayer book for Jews and Christians alike. In fact, the poetry's beauty and power to inspire worship still has modern songwriters spinning melodies around the sacred lyrics of the psalmists.

The purpose of this book is to bring the timeless comfort and inspiration of these psalms to your daily devotions in a unique way. Each of the 366 meditations is designed to help you focus on some aspect of a psalmist's prayer. Each includes a brief passage from the psalms, a related prayer from a modern-day perspective, and a final thought or quote that supports the meditation. And while daily entries take only a minute or two to read, the focus of the content is sure to remain with you throughout the day as a source of strength and encouragement.

From page to page, you'll encounter comfort, challenge, and inspiration. Very often you will hear a psalmist's call to trust in God and worship him because of his love, mercy, greatness, or faithfulness. What a wonderful way to begin, end, or interject something uplifting into your day!

With each successive reading, you will be reminded—or perhaps discover for the first time—how relevant these ancient

poems are to your own experience. The psalms included in this volume are filled with the cries of real people facing real life issues, just as you face them in your own daily lives.

While the prayers that follow each Scripture reading are an echo of the psalmist's heart cry, they bring a more intimate application to each passage The accompanying prayer is intended to give you a place to begin your own prayer, a prayer that resonates with a sincere and trusting faith and that is free to engage in open and honest conversation with the God who cares deeply for you.

While the poetry of the psalms is lovely, the prayers are not pious or pretentious. Their authenticity is a reminder that it doesn't take a special formula or level of spiritual growth to pray. Prayer is for anyone who finds a need to talk to God about anything. The ancients who wrote the passages on which you'll be meditating were not afraid to cry out to God, no matter what frame of heart and mind in which they found themselves. Perhaps your journey through the readings in this book will encourage you to imitate them. As they have shown us in their writings, fellowship with God is truly only a prayer away.

May you be blessed as you enjoy ever-increasing intimacy with the God of the ages over his timeless Word throughout the year ahead!

January

January 1

He put a new song in my mouth,
a song of praise to our God.
Many will see and fear,
and put their trust in the Lord.

Psalm 40:3

Lord, resolutions often fade with time. Sometimes I forget all about them, and sometimes I just give up on them, despite my best intentions. I do want to thank you, though, for this fresh start today, for this sense of a new beginning. And I was wondering if, instead of me trying to come up with some better approach to my life, you would come today and fill my heart and mind with reasons to be glad in you. I pray that these would overflow into songs of praise—songs that will continue throughout this year, lifting my own heart and encouraging others to look to you as well. In Jesus' name, I pray. Amen.

Music quickens time, she quickens us to the finest enjoyment of time.

—Thomas Mann, *The Magic Mountain*

January 2

*Happy are those
who do not follow the advice of the wicked . . . ;
but their delight is in the law of the Lord.
and on his law they meditate day and night.*

Psalm 1:1–2

*G*od, in this psalm I see the importance of the influences I choose each day. Thank you that even this time I am spending with you right now is a safeguard for my soul. The closer I stick to you, and the more I fill my mind with your Word, the more strength I have to do  the right thing. Please keep my heart and mind free of the clutter of compromise and half-truths. Thank you for the way your Word clarifies and simplifies my life. Counsel me with your truth today and every day. In your name, I pray. Amen.

There will be many moral junctures in the course of my day today. What I truly believe will be revealed in how I navigate each one.

January 3

You show me the path of life.
In your presence there is fullness of joy;
in your right hand are pleasures forevermore.

Psalm 16:11

Today, Lord, I've come into your presence again, just to be near you. Whether you have a new insight for me or just a reassurance of your care for me, I'm happy for the opportunity to commune with you right now. Help me stay close to you throughout the

day, and please keep your song of joy alive in my heart, fueled by gratitude for all the goodness you bring into my life. You are the one who makes my life truly worthwhile. May I remain in step with you along this blessing-filled path of life.

If we live by the Spirit,
let us also be guided by the Spirit.

—Galatians 5:25

January 4

O let the evil of the wicked come to an end,
but establish the righteous,
you who test the minds and hearts,
O righteous God.

Psalm 7:9

I understand that my sense of justice is not like yours, heavenly Father. Yours is perfect, while mine is limited and skewed, lopsided in favor of myself, and I never have all the illuminating facts and information to be able to judge exactly right where others are concerned. So I'm grateful, Lord, that you know precisely how to bring wickedness to light and to deal with it. And you know how to reward what is right and true and good. Help me live uprightly, truthfully, and honorably that I might be firmly established as one who walks in your ways.

Sir, I say that justice is truth in action.

—Benjamin Disraeli

January 5

The Lord is a stronghold for the oppressed,
a stronghold in times of trouble.

Psalm 9:9

Today, Lord, I feel oppressed by something or someone who seems bigger or stronger than I am or who seems indifferent to my needs or the needs of others. Please remind me not to be crushed in spirit or blinded by outrage. Instead, I ask that you would cut through my rising emotions, reminding me that you are bigger and stronger than  any power in heaven or on earth. Help me lean on you and find true comfort in you and protection from all forms of oppression.

A mighty fortress is our God,
A bulwark never failing;
Our helper, He amid the flood
Of mortal ills prevailing.

—Martin Luther, "A Mighty Fortress Is Our God"

January 6

Those who know your name put their trust in you,
for you, O Lord, have not forsaken those who seek you.

Psalm 9:10

Dear heavenly Father, you could give me no better comfort or assurance today than the promise that you, yourself, will remain with me. I can go forward into any situation or encounter—into the unknown, the dreaded, the eagerly anticipated . . . indeed, anything!—and I know that you will go with me through it. And then, on the other side of it, you'll still be there, ready to lead me onward. How good it is to belong to you and be kept safe by you!

Abide with me—fast falls the eventide;
The darkness deepens—Lord, with me abide!
When other helpers fail and comforts flee,
Help of the helpless, oh, abide with me!

—Henry F. Lyte, "Abide with Me"

January 7

O Lord, you will hear the desire of the meek;
you will strengthen their heart, you will incline your ear
to do justice for the orphan and the oppressed.

Psalm 10:17–18

You said, Lord Jesus, in your Sermon on the Mount that the meek—the humble and lowly—will inherit the earth. This promise you've made assures me that you see how the world's system works, that you are not indifferent to the way power often becomes corrupt and abusive, and that you have a plan to set things right. Thank you that you wield your ultimate power in a way that defends the weak and needy and protects the poor and helpless. Help me reflect your heart today by standing with those whose hearts need strengthening and by standing up for those who are longing for justice.

Humility is the one posture our souls can take that leaves our hands free to give and receive God's gifts of grace.

January 8

For you bless the righteous, O Lord;
you cover them with favor as with a shield.

Psalm 5:12

*S*ometimes the idea of righteousness fills
me with conflicting thoughts, heavenly
Father. I know I am not without sin, and yet I long to
do what is right. Thank you for placing this desire in
me and for fulfilling it with your own righteousness
through Jesus. Because you've forgiven my sin
through your Son and have graciously granted
me his righteousness as my own, I can claim this
promise of blessing today. By faith, I stand covered
with your favor, as with a shield. You're so good to
me, Lord! Thank you!

These exquisite robes of righteousness God has
provided for us are priceless. They fit perfectly,
and they are gifts of grace meant to be worn
daily and best accessorized with our
sincere joy and gratitude.

January 9

The promises of the Lord are promises that are pure,
silver refined in a furnace on the ground,
purified seven times.

Psalm 12:6

With you, dear Lord, a promise made is a promise kept. There is no question of your faithfulness in keeping your word. You have a perfect track record. That's why there is every reason for me to trust you today—to trust that you will keep your word and carry out your good purposes for my life as I keep my focus on you. Help me be patient and faithful as I wait for the fulfillment of your pure and perfect promises.

I claim God's promises for my life and look to their fulfillment, and rightly so, but that shows only the human perspective on them. God's perspective is that through His promises I will come to recognize His claim of ownership on me.

—Oswald Chambers

15

January 10

I will sing to the Lord,
because he has dealt bountifully with me.

Psalm 13:6

know I have a million reasons to sing today, O Lord! Please flood my mind with them even now. I have more reasons to be joyful than to be upset. Would you help me tune my heart and mind to a frequency of praise and worship today and avoid places on my emotional "dial" that tune in to channels of gloom and grumbling? I'll start by praising you for your bountiful grace and love. What would I do without them? Thank you, Father!

O, for a thousand tongues to sing
My great Redeemer's praise,
The glories of my God and King,
The triumphs of His grace!

—Charles Wesley, "O, for a Thousand Tongues"

January 11

I say to the Lord, "You are my Lord;
I have no good apart from you."

Psalm 16:2

My Lord, you are the one who watches over me and keeps me, the one who provides for me and gives me strength for each day, the one who stays with me and leads me toward those places that will bring me peace and blessing, including heaven where I will enjoy eternal life with you. What would I do without your loving presence in my life? My heart brims over with appreciation and love whenever I consider all the goodness you've poured out into my life.

Then Jesus said to the twelve,
"Do you also want to go away?"
Then Simon Peter answered Him,
"Lord, to whom shall we go?
You have the words of eternal life.
Also we have come to believe
and know that You are the Christ,
the Son of the living God."

—John 6:67–69 (NKJV)

January 12

I will both lie down and sleep in peace;
for you alone, O Lord, make me lie down in safety.

Psalm 4:8

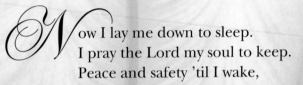

ow I lay me down to sleep.
I pray the Lord my soul to keep.
Peace and safety 'til I wake,
This I pray for Jesus' sake. Amen.

Lord, this childhood prayer calls me back to a childlike faith that can set aside the events of the day and embrace a restful night of sleep. Tonight when I lie down to sleep, remind me to leave my cares with you and to welcome the peace and safety you offer, day and night.

If I carry my worries with me and never lay them down, even to sleep, I become less and less able to meet the challenges they represent. Worry is a form of self-destruction, while faith is a means of daily renewal.

January 13

How intimately you care for me, omnipotent Father! I look at how big the world is and at how many things around me there are that can harm me. And yet, as fragile as I am,  I can move among life's dangers guarded by your watchfulness and sheltered by your protective love for me. I praise you for your tenderness, for your vigilance, and for making me your own child.

Under His wings I am safely abiding;
Though the night deepens and tempests are wild,
Still I can trust Him, I know He will keep me;
He has redeemed me, and I am His child.
Under His wings, under His wings,
Who from His love can sever?
Under His wings my soul shall abide,
Safely abide forever.

—William O. Cushing, "Under His Wings"

January 14

I call upon the Lord, who is worthy to be praised,
so I shall be saved from my enemies.

Psalm 18:3

I am uncomfortable referring to my antagonists as "enemies," Lord. The word *enemy* brings to mind political intrigues and military battles. But it's true that the people in my life who oppose me or who seek to harm me behave like enemies who have marked me as a target for their missions of ill will and their arrows of spite. What do I do, Lord? Since revenge is not an option, I'm calling out to you to defend me. Show me how to respond in each situation, whether I should turn and walk away or stand strong and demonstrate your strength and grace. Meanwhile, I'll keep praising you because you're in control: You do vindicate and are able to rescue me, and you will not let me be overcome by my "enemies."

A person may determine to be my enemy, but it does not follow that I am obligated to return the disfavor.

January 15

It is you who light my lamp;
the Lord, my God, lights up my darkness.

Psalm 18:28

ou really do light up my way, Lord! Whenever I feel myself groping in the darkness of uncertainty, confusion, or fear, I turn to you, and you enlighten my mind to the truth and show me the way through. I depend on your guiding Holy Spirit and your Word to illuminate my heart and mind with truth and wisdom for making right choices. How lost I would be without you! So I look to you again today to light my way, dear Lord. Please come and light up my darkness.

On dark nights while camping in the woods, one cannot walk even ten feet without tripping over something—a root or a rock—otherwise easily stepped over in the daytime. The smallest light in such thick darkness is a great blessing. What bit of light in my darkness can I be thankful for today?

January 16

For who is God except the Lord?
And who is a rock besides our God?—
the God who girded me with strength,
and made my way safe.

Psalm 18:31–32

My gracious God! You know I look to no false god of this world—not to money or material things, not to prestige or power, not to intellect or skill—to sustain my well-being and happiness. All of these earthly things can disappear in an instant from the landscape of my life. History clearly reveals that life's amenities can be here one day and gone the next. Not so with you, Lord. You are rock steady, eternal, and unfailing. You alone can keep me safe.

The true man trusts in a strength which is not his, and which he does not feel, does not even always desire.

—George MacDonald, *Unspoken Sermons*

January 17

*The Lord lives! Blessed be my rock,
and exalted be the God of my salvation.*

Psalm 18:46

*I*s there some way today, awesome God, that you can exalt your name through me? A way I might highlight the blessing of your salvation to those around me? I don't want to preach or push or pry in my desire for people to know how wonderful it is to belong to you. I just want to point to you in some encouraging and helpful way. Exalt yourself through me, I pray, in ways you see fit, in ways you know will be a benefit to those you've placed in my life and to those whom you send across my path.

When humanity is exalted for some accomplishment, it is not long before it topples from its pedestal. When God's name is exalted, however, there is no fear of disillusionment or disappointment.

January 18

Let the words of my mouth and the meditation of my heart
be acceptable to you,
O Lord, my rock and my redeemer.

Psalm 19:14

You see my focus, heavenly Father. You see where my mind and my mouth have been straying. I pray you will draw my thoughts to what is noble, true, encouraging, and loving right now so that my words may follow in kind. Please keep me from nursing hurts and grudges, keeping records of wrongs, and harboring criticisms against others. Set me free from any such destructive ways. And may my thoughts, words, attitudes, and actions please you.

Finally, beloved, whatever is true, whatever is honorable, whatever is just, whatever is pure, whatever is pleasing, whatever is commendable, if there is any excellence and if there is anything worthy of praise, think about these things.

—Philippians 4:8

January 19

The earth is the Lord's and all that is in it,
the world, and those who live in it.

Psalm 24:1

So often I think of myself as being autonomous and independent, or I think of myself in terms of my roles and relationships here on earth. The reality, dear Lord, is different than how I think and how I feel. The truth is that I belong to you. You made me, you sustain me, you have saved me, and you promise me that I am eternally yours. Help me live wholeheartedly for you today and not merely to please myself or those around me. Help me trust you by giving you your rightful place as Lord of my life.

Truth on the shelf of our lives is merely ornamental, but truth applied to our lives is powerful to transform us and influence those around us.

January 20

Who shall ascend the hill of the Lord? . . .
Those who have clean hands and pure hearts,
who do not lift up their souls to what is false.

Psalm 24:3–4

Examine my heart today, O God! I want to draw near to you. Open my eyes to those things in me that are false and that get in the way of our fellowship. Please give me the courage to abandon any lies to which I may be clinging. Whether I've fabricated them for self-protection, self-pity, self-aggrandizement, or any other self-seeking thing, please help me demolish each one, so that I may walk fully in the freedom of your right and true ways.

Repetition does not transform a lie into a truth.

—Franklin D. Roosevelt

January 21

Make me to know your ways, O Lord;
teach me your paths.

Psalm 25:4

Life with you is an adventure of learning, gracious Father! Help me look to each day with joyful anticipation. Fill me with a readiness to do your will and to change my ways if necessary so that I may walk in yours. Being with you, walking with you, and learning from you are what make my life worthwhile. Thank you for being such a patient and gentle teacher.

A good student listens, tries, learns, applies...
then turns to help others find their way.

January 22

Lead me in your truth, and teach me,
for you are the God of my salvation;
for you I wait all day long.

Psalm 25:5

Sometimes you seem silent when I'm begging for answers, Lord. Sometimes your silence seems like absence, but I know you are here. I know you are present with me. And your silence is neither a no nor a yes answer. In your silence, you call me to wait for you—to wait for your timing and to learn to trust you when I can't see what's ahead. So I'll sit still. I'll learn to wait patiently and appreciate the peace of your presence, knowing that you hold the past, present, and future in your hands. The truth is that I don't really need answers, Lord. I need you. Thank you for reminding me with your silence what is really necessary. I can rest in you while I wait.

We can always find God in the "waiting room" of our life, where he often has been waiting a long time for us to begin seeking him.

January 23

Do not remember the sins of my youth or my transgressions;
according to your steadfast love remember me.

Psalm 25:7

May God himself, the God of peace, sanctify you through and through. May your whole spirit, soul and body be kept blameless at the coming of our Lord Jesus Christ. The one who calls you is faithful and he will do it.... The grace of our Lord Jesus Christ be with you.

—1 Thessalonians 5:23–24, 28 (NIV)

The Lord's lovingkindnesses indeed never cease,
For His compassions never fail.
They are new every morning;
Great is Thy faithfulness.

—Lamentations 3:22–23 (NASB)

January 24

My eyes are ever toward the Lord,
for he will pluck my feet out of the net.

Psalm 25:15

My human instincts tell me to keep my eyes on those around me and to look out for what they might be doing or saying that could harm me. But your way, Lord, is counterintuitive; you call me to keep my eyes on you, for you promise to take care of me, keeping me safe. So I have a choice today: I can try to take care of myself, which is a stressful and often unsuccessful means of seeking safety, or I can trust you and enjoy a day of peace in your presence. I'm so thankful that I can choose you today.

If I've stepped into a "net" recently,
I must refuse to focus on my feet.
Turning my eyes heavenward,
I will call on the Lord and
trust him to save me.

January 25

Turn to me and be gracious to me,
for I am lonely and afflicted.

Psalm 25:16

*L*oving Father, you know I don't mind
being alone at times, but when loneliness
sets in, there's a sense of isolation and sadness that
overcomes me. You made me to be a relational
person, and yet sometimes you allow me to
experience a famine of relationships in my life.
It's at these times that I feel tremendous need for
company to soothe the ache and fill the void. Please
be my oasis in these times of drought. Be near me,
and remind me of your presence in ways I can grasp
and in ways that comfort and console me. Thank you
for always being with me.

[Jesus said,] "You will leave me all alone. Yet I
am not alone, for my Father is with me."

—John 16:32 (NIV)

January 26

Relieve the troubles of my heart,
and bring me out of my distress.

Psalm 25:17

*W*hile life's dark maze I tread
And griefs around me spread,
Be thou my guide;
Bid darkness turn to day,
Wipe sorrow's tears away,
Nor let me ever stray
From Thee aside.

—Ray Palmer, "My Faith Looks Up to Thee"

The troubles of my heart today are not too small
to be insignificant to God, nor are they too big
to be insurmountable for him. The mere fact
that my heart is troubled draws his attention,
his mercy, and his aid.

January 27

The Lord is my light and my salvation;
whom shall I fear?

Psalm 27:1

his psalm asks a rhetorical question, Lord, but I will answer it anyway: No one! I need fear no one with you leading the way in my life. Search my heart, Lord. Please show me ways I have been allowing my fear of others to displace my trust in you. Help me to not compromise my faith in any way today because of being afraid of what someone else might think about me or say to me or do to me. As you go before me, help me stand strong in the light of your salvation and not give an inch of ground to fear.

When I look to others for validation, I am continually battling either pride or fear; when I look to God, however, these battles cease, and the peace of trust prevails.

January 28

One thing I asked of the Lord,
that will I seek after:
to live in the house of the Lord
all the days of my life.

Psalm 27:4

I want to be where you are, dear Lord. I always want to be able to hear you—to always be communing with you. "Pray continually," your Word tells me. Please hold me in that place

of prayer. It is prayer that helps keep me near your "throne of grace" throughout the day. Thank you for inviting me here. In your presence—in the house of the Lord—is where I long to abide forever.

Let us then approach the throne of grace with confidence, so that we may receive mercy and find grace to help us in our time of need.

—Hebrews 4:16 (NIV)

January 29

"Come," my heart says, "seek his face!"
Your face, Lord, do I seek.

Psalm 27:8

When I wake up, you know my first thoughts, my Lord. You know what brings a smile to my face, what makes me groan, and what motivates me to throw the covers back and get going. But before I go to meet any of the pains or pleasures of the day, please remind me to look to you and to seek out your encouragement, counsel, and strength. How much better my days are when I take your hand and follow you through each hour! I seek your face right now and thank you for being here for me.

God is not hiding that we need to seek him. No, the problem is that we are often wandering far afield from where he waits for us. We have to leave our cities of selfishness, fairs of foolishness, and palaces of pride to find him where he is always waiting for us—in the quiet halls of prayer. We must seek him there.

January 30

Wait for the Lord;
be strong, and let your heart take courage;
wait for the Lord!

Psalm 27:14

Dear Lord, you know that waiting doesn't suit me when I think something should be happening right now. But thank you for reminding me today that I don't see the whole picture as you do. Help me to not simply endure as I wait, but rather to pluck up courage and live in an attitude of faith-filled anticipation of your good plan that is unfolding in your perfect timing. I want to praise you for that today too. Absolutely everything you do is excellent!

Waiting rooms of life are incubators of patience and trust, cocoons in which our struggling, earthbound spirits develop wings of faith.

January 31

Blessed be the Lord,
for he has heard the sound of my pleadings.

Psalm 28:6

Thank you for hearing my prayers, dear Lord, and for being attentive to my needs and requests. Help me remember to speak often of the ways you have brought me help, deliverance, blessing, and encouragement. I want my gratitude and praise to bless you, today and always. I love you!

My need to pray increases as I realize how small I am; my desire to pray increases as I realize how great God is.

37

February

February 1

*I will give to the Lord the thanks due to his righteousness,
and sing praise to the name of the Lord, the Most High.*

Psalm 7:17

Along with the psalmist, Lord, I thank you. You have blessed my life richly, and I live each day in gratitude. Each breath I take is a gift from you.  Each move I make stems from the power you bestow. All I am and all I have belong to you. Accept the expressions of my heart as songs of praise to you, my great and loving Lord. Let my entire life be an offering to you.

With gratitude in your hearts sing psalms, hymns, and spiritual songs to God. And whatever you do, in word or deed, do everything in the name of the Lord Jesus, giving thanks to God the Father through him.

—Colossians 3:16–17

February 2

Your steadfast love, O Lord, extends to the heavens,
your faithfulness to the clouds.

Psalm 36:5

*D*ear Lord, I rest in your steadfast love. It often overwhelms me how much you love me, even when I prove unlovable. Yet all my limits are met by your infinite commitment. I cannot fathom the extent of your love. On a clear night I gaze at starlight that began its journey thousands of years ago. Your love out-distances that. The sun sits 93 million miles off and gives me warmth, but your

love warms me even more. And even on a cloudy day I can imagine the showers of blessing you're storing up for me. Thank you so much, Lord, for your amazing love.

If you go outside today and see your shadow, you have six more weeks of opportunities to praise God for this winter season.

February 3

He gives snow like wool;
he scatters frost like ashes.
He hurls down hail like crumbs—
who can stand before his cold?
He sends out his word, and melts them;
he makes his wind blow, and the waters flow.

Psalm 147:16–18

I'm ready for springtime, Lord. I want to see growth and greenery, days getting longer, and breezes bringing warmth. Spring brings newness, and winter has me feeling old. But the psalmist reminds me that you are the author of both. With your creative power, you can freeze a stream and melt it. You can send a gale-force wind, and you can knit together a snowflake. I stand in wonder, awed by your amazing strength, and I ask you to work your wonders in me. Knit my life together with elegance. Melt my frozen streams of thought. Blow powerfully through all I do and say.

Though your sins are like scarlet,
they shall be like snow.

—Isaiah 1:18

February 4

This God—his way is perfect;
the promise of the Lord proves true;
he is a shield for all who take refuge in him.

Psalm 18:30

Great God, I praise and honor you for keeping your promises. You have said that you would be with us always and that you would give us life and peace and protect us from harm. You have acknowledged that tough times would come, but you have promised to meet us there, to share your bountiful resources with us, to help us through the crises, and to be our refuge. Thank you, Lord, for being with us.

Often the Lord has to protect us from our own crazy schemes. We might think we know where we're going and how to get there, but he has a better idea.

February 5

Sing to God, sing praises to his name;
lift up a song to him who rides upon the clouds—
his name is the Lord—
be exultant before him.

Psalm 68:4

Dear Lord, today I lift up my heart and voice to praise you. You are a great God. I am privileged to be called your child. In the midst of my daily challenges, I consider that fact—that I am your child—and I rejoice in it. It's fun to imagine you, as the psalmist says, "riding upon the clouds." I know that's a reference to your greatness, your power over all creation, but could I see it in a more literal way? You see, my days aren't always bright and sunny. There are frequent "clouds" of disappointment and struggle. Yet I find that in these times when I need you most, you ride in to help me. You are the Lord not only in good times but also on cloudy days.

My brothers and sisters, whenever you face trials of any kind, consider it nothing but joy, because you know that the testing of your faith produces endurance; and let endurance have its full effect, so that you may be mature and complete, lacking in nothing.

—James 1:2–4

February 6

Make a joyful noise to God, all the earth;
sing the glory of his name;
give to him glorious praise.

Psalm 66:1–2

A careening car, a passing train, a whining child. A clap of thunder, the first splats of rain on the roof, the flap of windshield wipers. A cat's purr, a faucet's drip, a refrigerator's hum. My cell phone ringing, the microwave beeping, the alarm clock waking me. Lord, you have created a world full of noise, and our machines have made it even noisier. These sounds can alert me and annoy me, scare me and soothe me. But what if all these noises are part of a music I don't yet understand? Could they all be parts of a symphony of praise for the Creator? You made electrons and sound waves and eardrums and voiceboxes, and now they all celebrate your creativity. Let my voice join the chorus, Lord.

If you can sing, sing. If you can't carry a tune, let the Spirit carry it for you. We don't need to make a symphony to the Lord, just a joyful *noise.*

February 7

I will exult and rejoice in your steadfast love,
because you have seen my affliction;
you have taken heed of my adversities.

Psalm 31:7

My Lord, sometimes I feel all alone, as if no one really knows what I'm going through or no one cares. Yes, there are people in my life, and some of them treat me nicely, but there are times when even their kindnesses aren't enough. I feel isolated, abandoned, up against overwhelming obstacles with little or no support. But a psalm like this one gets me grounded again. You have seen my affliction. You understand my adversity. In your divine knowledge, you know exactly what's going on, and you promise me your steadfast love. Even before anything changes, it's a comfort to know that *you* know. It's a blessing to sense your presence beside me. And now I ask for your strength to overcome any obstacle.

Of all the great things God does for us, one of the greatest is that he *sees* us in our need.

February 8

I will instruct you and teach you the way you should go;
I will counsel you with my eye upon you.

Psalm 32:8

each me, dear Lord. I am a willing pupil. I sit in the front row, textbook open, with a shiny apple on my desk. Well, not always. I'll admit

that sometimes I'm slouched in the back row, chewing gum, unprepared, hoping you won't call on me. But you are my teacher, and you always find a way to get through to me, whether I'm eager or reluctant. Thank you for your instruction. Keep showing me the way to live. Keep guiding me step by step.

Wouldn't it be great to have a spiritual GPS, some portable system that would show us where God wanted us to go? Well, we do have one. It's called the Holy Spirit.

46

February 9

Yours is the day, yours also the night;
you established the luminaries and the sun.
You have fixed all the bounds of the earth;
you made summer and winter.

Psalm 74:16–17

Summer and winter and springtime
  and harvest,
Sun, moon, and stars in their courses above
Join with all nature in manifold witness
To thy great faithfulness, mercy, and love.

Great is thy faithfulness! Great is thy faithfulness!
Morning by morning new mercies I see.
All I have needed thy hand hath provided.
Great is thy faithfulness, Lord, unto me.

—Thomas O. Chisholm, "Great Is Thy Faithfulness"

God called the light Day, and the darkness he
called Night. And there was evening and
there was morning, the first day.

—Genesis 1:5

February 10

I sought the Lord, and he answered me,
and delivered me from all my fears.
Look to him, and be radiant;
so your faces shall never be ashamed.

Psalm 34:4–5

The world can be a scary place, heavenly Father. With terrorism, disease, and economic uncertainty, there's not much we can count on anymore. Except you. I fear for my own health, my family's well-being, and the state of my country, but I bring these fears to you. Fill me with faith. Help me trust you for true security. Let my life radiate with confidence in your love and power.

Do not fear, for I am with you,
do not be afraid, for I am your God;
I will strengthen you, I will help you,
I will uphold you with my victorious right hand.

—Isaiah 41:10

February 11

Happy are those who make
the Lord their trust,
who do not turn to the proud,
to those who go astray after false gods.

Psalm 40:4

Precious Lord, there are various "false gods" in this world, and I'll admit that I have strayed after some of them. Money is a big one. I keep thinking that my problems will be solved if I just get enough money, but that's not true, is it? I chase after pleasure and success and entertainment as if they gave my life meaning. My house, my car, or my closet might as well be "graven images." But you continue to remind me that these things don't bring ultimate satisfaction. You are the only God worth trusting. I find fulfillment only in you.

You shall have no other gods before me.

—Exodus 20:3

February 12

He has pity on the weak and the needy,
and saves the lives of the needy.

Psalm 72:13

Mighty Lord and Savior, I love you for your compassion. Many times in my life I have cried out to you in great need of one kind or another, and you have responded. I don't know why you would care about my needs, but you do. Now I ask that you would open my heart to reach out to others around me. Make me sensitive to their needs. Help me find creative ways to meet their needs. Give me courage to cross boundaries if necessary. Most of all, give me your heart to extend your love to others.

The problem with climbing the ladder of success is that we keep looking up, envying those above us, when we should be reaching down to help those below.

February 13

For as the heavens are high above the earth,
so great is his steadfast love toward those who fear him.

Psalm 103:11

Could we with ink the ocean fill,
        And were the skies of parchment made,
Were every stalk on earth a quill,
And every man a scribe by trade,
To write your love, O God above,
Would drain the ocean dry.
Nor could the scroll contain the whole,
Though stretched from sky to sky.

—Adapted from "The Love of God" by Frederick M.
Lehman, based on medieval Jewish poem *Haddamut*,
                by cantor Meir Ben Isaac Neharai

For I am convinced that neither death, nor life,
nor angels, nor rulers, nor things present, nor
things to come, nor powers, nor height, nor
depth, nor anything else in all creation, will
be able to separate us from the love
of God in Christ Jesus our Lord.

—Romans 8:38–39

February 14

I love the Lord, because he has heard
my voice and my supplications.
Because he inclined his ear to me,
therefore I will call on him as long as I live.

Psalm 116:1–2

My heart is filled with love for you, dear Lord. I can't begin to express the depth of my feelings. You have created me and re-created me. You have forgiven me and saved me. You give me joy each day and hope for the days ahead. When I call upon you in a time of need, you hear my prayer. You come close to me and whisper the assurance of your love. Thank you, Lord, for listening to me. I love you.

God is love, and those who abide in love
abide in God, and God abides in them.

—1 John 4:16

February 15

Those who love me, I will deliver;
I will protect those who know my name.

Psalm 91:14

Jesus, the very thought of thee
    with sweetness fills my breast,
    But sweeter far thy face to see,
and in thy presence rest.

O hope of every contrite heart,
O joy of all the meek,
To those who fall, how kind thou art!
How good to those who seek! . . .

Jesus, our only joy be thou,
as thou our prize wilt be.
Jesus, be thou our glory now,
and through eternity.

—Bernard of Clairvaux

Love has hands to help others. It has feet to
hasten to the poor and needy. It has eyes to see
misery and want. It has ears to hear the sighs
and sorrows of men. This is what love looks like.

—Augustine

53

February 16

O grant us help against the foe,
for human help is worthless.

Psalm 108:12

People have consistently let me down, Lord, and I'm tired of it. I feel hurt right now, and I need your help. I'm not saying I'm perfectly dependable myself; I'm only human. But my problems require a higher level of assistance. Will you bring your divine power and wisdom into my situation? Give me strength against laziness and complacency. Help me fight the temptations that pull me down. Quiet the naysayers. Calm the backbiters. Grant me the determination and confidence I need to do your work in this world.

All people are grass, their constancy
is like the flower of the field. . . .
The grass withers, the flower fades;
but the word of our God
will stand forever.

—Isaiah 40:6, 8

February 17

With a freewill offering I will sacrifice to you;
I will give thanks to your name, O Lord, for it is good.

Psalm 54:6

Dear Lord, I want to give you something, a token of my thanks and love. In days of old, they brought sacrifices to the Temple, gifts of grain or livestock. I suppose I can give you money, donating to my church or a charity, but that quickly becomes a mathematical transaction, just another bill to pay. I want to give you something meaningful, something sacrificial. My time? Maybe. My creative effort? Would I dare to take a chance on some artistic offering, not being confident about the outcome? Or could I show an extravagant kindness to one of "the least of these," the poor and needy? What kind of gift do you want from me, Lord? Please show me.

Every gift we give God is our heart, just wrapped up in something different each time. Our money, our service, even our praises— these are just containers for the loving gratitude of our hearts.

February 18

For God alone my soul waits in silence;
from him comes my salvation.
He alone is my rock and my salvation,
my fortress; I shall never be shaken.

Psalm 62:1–2

Sometimes, Lord, I just need to get away from it all—to be quiet and rest. Thank you for providing a place of rest. Life spins so quickly that I can't always keep up. I start to worry about what might happen. Those worries then add stress to my life, affecting the way I work and the way I relate to others. Friendships get frayed, mistakes get made, and I have even more to worry about. So right now I'm quieting down, and I'm turning to you for help. I trust you to provide the deliverance I need.

Do not worry about anything, but in everything by prayer and supplication with thanksgiving let your requests be made known to God. And the peace of God, which surpasses all understanding, will guard your hearts and your minds in Christ Jesus.

—Philippians 4:6–7

February 19

*At an acceptable time, O God,
in the abundance of your steadfast love, answer me.
With your faithful help rescue me
from sinking in the mire.*

Psalm 69:13–14

Dear Lord, I usually track quite well with the psalmist. The details are different, but the essential situations still exist—trouble, enemies, and a need for deliverance in tough times. This particular psalm is the story of my life, too. So I have to laugh a little when the psalmist cries out for help "at an acceptable time." As I picture it, the psalmist is sinking in quicksand, about to be swallowed up, and the prayer is: "When you have a minute, Lord, if it's not too much trouble, would you think about saving me?" I laugh, but then I realize that time is often the issue. I pray for all sorts of things that I want *now,* and I complain when you don't immediately respond. Maybe, in your wisdom, you're just waiting for "an acceptable time."

God has all the time in the
world, and then some.

February 20

You forgave the iniquity of your people;
you pardoned all their sin.

Psalm 85:2

I humbly bow before your throne,
    Ashamed of things that I have done.
    How could you ever look at me again?
My promises have come to naught.
I haven't lived the way I ought.
    That's not a fitting way to treat a friend.
I will not dare to seek your face.
I plead for mercy, love, and grace.
    Perhaps you could restore some tiny part?
You lift me up and take my hand,
With words I'll never understand,
    And let forgiveness flower from your heart.

We don't earn forgiveness. We can't. Excuses
don't make us more forgivable, but less.
The only way to find forgiveness is
to admit we've done wrong.

February 21

Sing praises to the Lord with the lyre,
with the lyre and the sound of melody.
With trumpets and the sound of the horn
make a joyful noise before the King, the Lord.

Psalm 98:5–6

What instruments do I have to praise you with, dear Lord? The whoosh of the photocopier as I do my office work? The gurgle of the coffeemaker in the kitchen? Perhaps even the annoying sound in the car engine could join in the symphony of praise. I want to gather elements of my entire life and offer them to you. I don't stop being your child when I work, or when I drive, or when I

sip a steaming cup of coffee. The music comes from every aspect of my world, and I offer it all to you as my paean of praise.

Then the prophet Miriam, Aaron's sister, took a tambourine in her hand; and all the women went out after her with tambourines and with dancing. And Miriam sang to them: "Sing to the Lord, for he has triumphed gloriously."

—Exodus 15:20–21

February 22

I bless the Lord who gives me counsel;
in the night also my heart instructs me.
I keep the Lord always before me;
because he is at my right hand, I shall not be moved.

Psalm 16:7–8

My Lord, I think of the various "counselors" I've had in my life. It's a mixed bag. Parents, friends, ministers, teachers, coaches, camp counselors, and guidance counselors in school. Some of them brought true wisdom, and I believe you used them to guide me in your path. Others had different motives. Some were fully invested, caring deeply about me. Others were more interested in hearing themselves talk, and they didn't hang around long enough to see the results. But you, Lord, are a counselor who cares, stays close to me, and knows me deeply. Keep counseling me, day and night, and I'll keep listening for your voice.

His Holy Spirit speaks to us deep in our hearts
and tells us that we are God's children.

—Romans 8:16 (NLT)

February 23

I lift up my eyes to the hills—
from where will my help come?
My help comes from the Lord,
who made heaven and earth.

Psalm 121:1–2

*A*ll my life, Lord, I've been lifting up my eyes in various directions, hoping to find the help I need. And I'm not the only one. A career path, a financial plan, popularity, home and family. I know they're not bad things, but we tend to put them up on a pedestal and expect them to save us. How many were counting on savings accounts and retirement plans when the economy went south? That's a hard lesson to learn. And when those idols crumble, many of us turn to various escapes— alcohol, drugs, and so on. You know the escapes I've tried, but I keep coming back to you. Where does my help come from? From the loving Lord who made me. I put my trust in you.

In the psalmist's time, "the hills" were where idol-worshippers had their sacred groves. Help comes, not from the hills, but from the One who *made* the hills.

February 24

I lie down and sleep;
I wake again, for the Lord sustains me.

Psalm 3:5

At last! What a day it has been! I thought I'd never get to this moment, dear Lord. Thank you for the ways you were there for me today. I really sensed your presence throughout the day.

Please work things out for me tomorrow, too. And please give me a good night's sleep. Let's talk again in the morning. Amen.

Sleep . . . knits up the raveled sleeve of care . . . sore labor's bath, balm of hurt minds . . . chief nourisher in life's feast.

—William Shakespeare, *Macbeth*

February 25

Young men and women alike,
old and young together!
Let them praise the name of the Lord,
for his name alone is exalted;
his glory is above earth and heaven.

Psalm 148:12–13

Dear Lord, you know I have my ways of worshipping you. There are certain songs I like and certain actions I'm accustomed to. There's a certain style I've learned that really makes me feel close to you. But I know you're a big God, and you have a lot of worshippers. Different ages and genders, and also different cultures—everyone can bring their own styles to worship. It's not always easy for me to worship you in someone else's style, but I can try. That's what it means to be a congregation, I guess—to be a family, to be the people of God.

I will pour out my spirit on all flesh; your sons and your daughters shall prophesy, your old men shall dream dreams, and your young men shall see visions.

—Joel 2:28

February 26

Why, O Lord, do you stand far off?
Why do you hide yourself in times of trouble?

Psalm 10:1

Are you there, Lord? Are you? At times it seems that you're distant, and I'm not sure why. Have I strayed away from you? I don't think so. Have I offended you in some way? If so, I don't know how. I just don't feel the closeness we used to have. Is it just me, or is there a problem here? Maybe you don't want me to take you for granted. But because you have promised to be here for me *always*, I'm going to trust you to be with me, even when you're silent. If I have sinned, Lord, please let me know. If not, then just keep guiding me, even if that guidance is subtle. And please don't stop watching over me.

Like any muscle, faith gets stronger
when it meets stronger resistance.

February 27

The law of the Lord is perfect,
reviving the soul;
the decrees of the Lord are sure,
making wise the simple.

Psalm 19:7

Revive my soul, dear Lord, as I open your Word. Speak to me in clear, inspiring ways. Breathe new life into my old life. Show me how to live. Encourage me. Move me into new enterprises that will serve you. Lead me into adventures in my activities and relationships. Give me the courage to try some things that have never been tried before. Overcome the barriers I put up, and let your awesome power explode through me.

Indeed, the word of God is living and active, sharper than any two-edged sword, piercing until it divides soul from spirit, joints from marrow; it is able to judge the thoughts and intentions of the heart.

—Hebrews 4:12

February 28

The Lord sits enthroned over the flood;
the Lord sits enthroned as king forever.
May the Lord give strength to his people!
May the Lord bless his people with peace!

Psalm 29:10–11

Y ou are my King, O Lord. Blessed be your name. I magnify you, telling of your greatness. You rule the earth with your loving power. You dwell in your people and whisper words of peace and guidance. You are immense and intimate at the same time, the Creator of all, yet friend to the needy. I will praise you as long as I live.

God is an infinite circle
whose center is everywhere
and whose circumference is nowhere.

—Augustine

February 29

All my bones shall say,
"O Lord, who is like you?
You deliver the weak
from those too strong for them,
the weak and needy from those who despoil them."

Psalm 35:10

When I am weak, Lord, you give me strength.
When I'm embattled, you fight for me.
When I am tired, Lord, you give me rest.
When I am anxious, you calm me.
When I am clueless, you give me light.
When I mess up, you forgive me.
When I'm defeated, you lift up my head.
You lift up my heart and lead on.

"Come to me, all you that are weary and are carrying heavy burdens, and I will give you rest. Take my yoke upon you, and learn from me; for I am gentle and humble in heart, and you will find rest for your souls. For my yoke is easy, and my burden is light."

—Matthew 11:28–30

March

March 1

O Lord, our Sovereign,
how majestic is your name in all the earth!

Psalm 8:1

Joyful, joyful, we adore thee,
  God of glory, Lord of love;
Hearts unfold like flowers before thee,
  Opening to the sun above.
Melt the clouds of sin and sadness,
  Drive the dark of doubt away;
Giver of immortal gladness,
  Fill us with the light of day.

—Henry van Dyke, "Joyful, Joyful, We Adore Thee"

The queens and kings of earth borrow their majesty from God's hand. No mortal, with all his might, can cause even a blade of grass to grow, and yet the grandeur of the mountains on which the meadows flourish is the result of a mere few words spoken by God!

March 2

When I look at your heavens, the work of your fingers,
the moon and the stars that you have established;
what are human beings . . .
that you care for them?

Psalm 8:3–4

I am in awe of the depth of your love for
me, dear Lord. You say in your Word that
your thoughts toward me are too many to count.
You watch over my life with such care and precision.
If you counted me as mere matter in the universe, I
would be but a mote of dust. Instead, you count me
as your child and crown me with value and dignity by
that distinction. I am humbled and delighted all at
once. I love belonging to you and being invited into
fellowship with you.

Wonder looks up to unnumbered stars,
In unfathomed deeps of midnight.
This faraway fire stirs my desire
For the unchanging face of Your light.
And I sing, "O Lord, great are Your works;
The moon and the stars speak of You!"
O Lord, my heart has heard,
And I long to say, "I love You."

—Christine Dallman

March 3

By your favor, O Lord,
you . . . established me as a strong mountain.

Psalm 30:7

Your grace and your favor in my life have steadied me and caused me to grow strong in gratitude and trust. I have learned much in the hard times of life, but no less significant are the lessons I have learned when you have shown me your goodness. I have learned not to attribute my successes and blessings to myself; I have learned to acknowledge you as the source of every good gift I have. I want to praise you for this inner strength that carries me through each day. No matter what circumstances I may encounter, I am strong in you.

Is there a mountain at which you can gaze today, whether out your window or in a picture? Let it remind you of how firmly God has established your faith by his grace.

March 4

Sing praises to the Lord, O you his faithful ones,
and give thanks to his holy name.

Psalm 30:4

My Lord, even when I don't feel like singing, please remind me of how much you deserve to be praised. And if I am slow to respond with my own voice, help me express my song along with the help of others who are singing your praises—whether in a worship service or with a song on the radio. If it takes an mp3 player to get my praises flowing, then use that technology to help me glorify you. Don't let me miss an opportunity to sing your praises today. You're truly deserving of every bit of worship that I can lift to you.

It doesn't matter if our singing is angelic or we're just plain tone deaf, God's ear listens, not for right notes but for a spirit of truth in our praises. With this kind of worship, he is well pleased.

March 5

You have turned my mourning into dancing;
you have taken off my sackcloth
and clothed me with joy.

Psalm 30:11

s winter's mournful ways begin to dissolve and spring's joyful face emerges, almighty Lord, I recall that you are the one who made the seasons of the earth, which so aptly reflect the seasons of my own life. From within times of mourning, it seems as if things will never be different, that my heart will remain frozen with grief and clouded over with pain. But each successive day moves me steadily, though often imperceptibly, toward a new season of heart, soul, and mind. Thank you for your sure and gentle ways that teach me—when I've forgotten how—to dance once again.

Never let anything so fill you with sorrow as to
make you forget the joy of the Christ risen.

—Mother Teresa, *A Gift for God*

March 6

*Happy are those whose transgression is forgiven,
whose sin is covered.*

Psalm 32:1

ather in heaven!
Hold not our sins
up against us but hold us
up against our sins, so that
the thought of Thee when it
wakens in our soul, and each
time it wakens, should not
remind us of what we have
committed but of what Thou
didst forgive, not of how we
went astray but of how Thou
didst save us.

—Søren Kierkegaard, "Hold Not Our Sins"

Today I will remember to receive God's grace in
the way it is offered—as a precious gift.

March 7

Therefore let all who are faithful
offer prayer to you;
at a time of distress, the rush of mighty waters
shall not reach them.

Psalm 32:6

*I*t's one of the great blessings of belonging to you, heavenly Father, that I can remain calm and certain in a world of chaos and uncertainty. It's not that I am never touched by the

ills of living in a fallen world; certainly I am! But it's that they don't carry me away into utter ruin and despair because you hold me fast.

We should never be afraid or hesitant to send SOS prayers to our heavenly Father. God is just as attentive to our desperate cries for help as he is to our more thought-filled prayers lifted during "quiet times" with him.

March 8

*Be glad in the Lord and rejoice, O righteous,
and shout for joy, all you upright in heart.*

Psalm 32:11

I know it's true that different people
worship in different ways, my Lord.
What you look for in our worship—however it is
expressed—is that we worship in "spirit and in
truth." It's wonderful, though, to read this invitation
in the psalms to express our joy
in you with literal shouts of
rejoicing. I pray that you will
make my joy in you overflow
today in such a way that I
might be inclined to shout my
praise to you even now.

Movies often portray those who are devout as
sour, dour, killjoy types, but in "real life,"
most of the genuinely joyful people we've
met have been those who know a life
of humble devotion to God.

March 9

For the word of the Lord is upright,
and all his work is done in faithfulness.

Psalm 33:4

*D*ear Lord, thank you for your Word and your work in my life. Your Word has kept me from straying far from you and has encouraged and renewed my faith again and again. And your work of grace continues to transform me within. Day by day, you are as faithful as the sunrise. How good you are!

Scripture says that though people fall, God's Word will remain firm and never fall. Anyone who falls will be able to stand up again on the strength of God's Word.

—Martin Luther, *Faith Alone: A Daily Devotional*

March 10

He loves righteousness and justice;
the earth is full of the steadfast love of the Lord.

Psalm 33:5

*M*y heavenly Father, thank you for surrounding me with all the blessings that flow from your love in action—in this world and in my life. As I move through this day, cause me to walk in your righteousness and justice. May your steadfast love steady me as I reach out, not only to those who will be appreciative of your grace but also to those who will not be. For the glory of your name, I pray. Amen.

He has showed you, O man, what is good.
And what does the Lord require of you?
To act justly and to love mercy and
to walk humbly with your God.

—Micah 6:8 (NIV)

March 11

*The angel of the Lord encamps
around those who fear him, and delivers them.*

Psalm 34:7

*D*ear Lord, I'm humbled by all the ways you guard my life. I have seen your intervention come when I've needed it, and I know without a doubt that you are watching over me. You

even send your ministering angels to bring a unique kind of watching care when I need it. Fill my heart with faith in your ability to deliver me from harm by whatever means you choose.

Angels do not seek our praise, our worship, or our prayers. Such things belong to the Creator.

March 12

O taste and see that the Lord is good;
happy are those who take refuge in him.

Psalm 34:8

What flavor of your goodness will I taste today, Lord? You are always blessing my life with good things. I savor your grace and mercy. Your love is a feast. I always want seconds of your kindness. And your recipe for peace is not to be outdone by anyone. I am happy to be invited to such a banquet.

He brings me to the banquet hall and everyone can see how much he loves me.

—Song of Solomon 2:4 (TLB)

March 13

O fear the Lord, you his holy ones,
for those who fear him have no want.

Psalm 34:9

*D*ear Lord, I understand that by "fearing" you don't mean cowering or abject terror. You mean a proper respect, honor, and reverence for who you are that cause me to fervently desire to obey you and stay in right relationship with you. And I do want to properly fear you. But in a culture where flippancy, disrespect, and selfishness are prevalent, I ask you to help me regard you as I ought—to honor you well, because I love you so much.

The Book of Proverbs tells us that the fear of the Lord is a catalyst for many good things in our lives: It is the beginning of wisdom, knowledge, and understanding; it is a fountain of life and prolongs life; it is a strong confidence and refuge; it keeps us from evil; it provides peace of mind; it even brings riches, honor, and life!

March 14

The young lions suffer want and hunger,
but those who seek the Lord lack no good thing.

Psalm 34:10

*W*onderful Father, help me not turn an envious eye to those around me who have strength, beauty, success, riches... or any of those "powers" the world values so much. Humans left to our own devices eventually wear out: Our beauty fades, our wealth dwindles, and our strength ebbs away. No, Lord, I won't look to those earthbound things for significance, worth, value, or strength. I will seek you and look to you for everything I need. Only in you is eternal life and ample provision for this temporal part of life's journey.

When I was a boy I used to think that *strong* meant having big muscles, great physical power; but the longer I live, the more I realize that real strength has much more to do with what is *not* seen.

—Fred Rogers, *The World According to Mister Rogers: Important Things to Remember*

March 15

The eyes of the Lord are on the righteous,
and his ears are open to their cry.

Psalm 34:15

What a comfort to realize that you, dear Lord, always have your eyes and ears open, not just in a general way, but specifically to watch over me and to listen for my cries! There have been times in my life when I thought of you as being indifferent toward me. There have been times when I've even thought you were rejecting me. But I realize now how wrong I was—that it was just my small perspective leading me to those wrong conclusions. I rejoice today in your attentiveness toward me, and in faith I will look to you and call out to you throughout this day and every day.

The God who is attentive to every detail of our lives—even down to the trivial, such as knowing the number of hairs on our heads at any given moment—will not fail to give his loving attention to the things that most deeply concern us.

March 16

The Lord looks down from heaven on humankind
to see if there are any who are wise,
who seek after God.

Psalm 14:2

After this manner therefore pray ye:
Our Father which art in heaven,
Hallowed be thy name.
Thy kingdom come.
Thy will be done in earth, as it is in heaven.
Give us this day our daily bread.
And forgive us our debts, as we forgive our
debtors.
And lead us not into
temptation, but deliver us from evil:
For thine is the kingdom, and
the power, and the glory, for ever.
Amen.

—Matthew 6:9–13 (KJV)

Seeking God and his kingdom above
all else is the wisest investment
we will ever make in this life.

March 17

*As for the holy ones in the land, they are the noble,
in whom is all my delight.*

Psalm 16:3

*L*ord, be with us this day,
    Within us to purify us;
Above us to draw us up;
Beneath us to sustain us;
Before us to lead us;
Behind us to restrain us;
Around us to protect us.

—St. Patrick

Saints are made, not by their own deeds or
piety, but by the saving grace of God alone.

March 18

O Lord, who may abide in your tent?
Who may dwell on your holy hill?
Those who walk blamelessly, and do what is right,
and speak the truth from their heart.

Psalm 15:1–2

*I*n the little sin "allowances" I sometimes make for myself, loving Father—allowances to lie or cheat or steal, even in the smallest of ways—I undermine our fellowship and estrange myself from being at peace with you in your presence. There is nothing in this world that is worth that sacrifice. Please wake me up today to the things I am doing that are not pure and right and true. May your Spirit bring a sense of grief to my heart at the wrong of such things. Then I will confess them and seek to forsake them and be reconciled to you at once. In Jesus' name, I pray. Amen.

Catch for us the foxes, the little foxes that ruin the vineyards, our vineyards that are in bloom.

—Song of Solomon 2:15 (NIV)

March 19

For the Lord is righteous,
he loves righteous deeds;
the upright shall behold his face.

Psalm 11:7

The promise of being face to face with you one day, dear Lord, is something I hold tightly to in this life of ups and downs. Right now I must take all that I know about you on faith. There is a great body of evidence that assures me that my faith is resting on solid ground, but still I cannot wait for the day when what I have faith in becomes visible. I want to behold the one who fashioned me in my mother's womb, who saved me with his own life, and who has cared for me by his great love. I want to see you and embrace you. How I love you!

Only faintly now I see Him,
With the darkling veil between;
But a blessed day is coming
When His glory shall be seen.
Face to face shall I behold him,
Far beyond the starry sky;
Face to face in all His glory,
I shall see Him by and by.

—Carrie E. Breck, "Face to Face"

87

March 20

But who can detect their errors?
Clear me from hidden faults....
[D]o not let them have dominion over me.
Then I shall be blameless,
and innocent of great transgression.

Psalm 19:12–13

*F*ather in
Heaven!
Reawaken conscience in
our breast. Make us bend
the ear of the spirit to
Thy voice, so that we may
perceive Thy will for us

in its clear purity as it is in heaven, pure of our false
worldly wisdom, unstifled by the voice of passion;
keep us vigilant.

– Søren Kierkegaard, "To Know Thy Will"

We can become unaware of (or grow calloused
to) things that have crept into our lives over
time—sinful thoughts, attitudes, and actions—
that work against our relationship with God.
That's why self-examination under the direction
of God's Spirit can be vitally important
to our spiritual growth.

March 21

The Lord is near to the brokenhearted,
and saves the crushed in spirit.

Psalm 34:18

In the middle of my pain, loving Father,
sometimes there are no words I can bring
to you—only groans of anguish, tears of sorrow, and

the silence of suffering
in which I can sense
you sitting with me, also
silent. But your presence
has its own language of
communion with my
broken spirit. You don't
despise my grief; you
share in it with me.
Thank you for always
being here with me no
matter what.

Though the sorrow in our hearts causes us to
tremble and weep, the Lord holds us
tightly in his comforting embrace.

March 22

The Lord redeems the life of his servants;
none of those who take refuge in him will be condemned.

Psalm 34:22

When I am unfaithful to you, almighty God, when I fail to serve you well, I sometimes feel frustrated with myself and think you feel the same way. But you don't! You simply call me back to yourself, back to the rivers of your redemption. There I can be washed clean and there you can turn the tides of my wayward self-seeking back to seeking your kingdom and your righteousness. Thank you for your tireless, redeeming love, dear Father. I take refuge in you today and always.

There is therefore now no condemnation to those who are in Christ Jesus, who do not walk according to the flesh, but according to the Spirit.

—Romans 8:1 (NKJV)

March 23

How precious is your steadfast love, O God!
All people may take refuge in the shadow of your wings.

Psalm 36:7

here is no one you exclude from your
invitation to come to you, divine Lord.
That includes me! So I come gratefully today,
joyfully, to find a place of shelter in your protective
love. I know I will encounter ups and downs, but I

also know that as I
continue to entrust
myself to your care,
the "downs" will
be buffered by the
knowledge that I am
perfectly safe and
truly cared for by you.

God's love is such that I am never disqualified
from receiving it. It is always accessible to me.
Only my unwillingness to accept it from him
can ever deprive me of its full benefits.

March 24

Do not fret because of the wicked;
do not be envious of wrongdoers,
for they will soon fade like the grass,
and wither like the green herb.

Psalm 37:1–2

*L*ord, it's hard not to get upset when wickedness seems to prevail. I hear about horrors in the news; I learn of crimes in my community; I am told of injustices in government; I feel the effects of evildoers, even in my personal life. But you say, in your Word, that wickedness is short-lived and that those who insist on walking in crooked paths will soon disappear: Here today, gone tomorrow. Wow! That's sobering. Help me trust your love of righteousness and justice that is able to set things right. It's a good thing for me to hate evil, but remind me to pray for those who have become ensnared by it.

No man is condemned for anything he has done: he is condemned for continuing to do wrong. He is condemned for not coming out of the darkness, for not coming into the light.

—George MacDonald, *Unspoken Sermons*

March 25

Trust in the Lord, and do good;
so you will live in the land, and enjoy security.

Psalm 37:3

At times, almighty God, evil seems prevalent in the world. But I know that evil will not prevail. You prevail in all things. So I'll keep my focus on you, and do what is right, even if it seems like an exercise in futility and even though it seems as if doing wrong

would get me ahead and doing right will cause me grief. I will choose to do good, entrusting my well-being and security to you.

Those who do good can look at themselves in the mirror, look others in the eye, and look heavenward in prayer without shame.

March 26

*Take delight in the Lord,
and he will give you the desires of your heart.*

Psalm 37:4

When was the last time I delighted in you, my Lord? Was it when I thrilled at some bit of simple but profound wisdom in your Word? Was it when I sensed your presence with me in some corner of my day? Or when I stopped to linger appreciatively over some aspect of this world you've created? Everything about you delights me—even the fact that you sometimes correct me, because I know you care for me. There will be reasons today for me to delight in you, as well. Help me not miss them, for *you* are the deepest desire of my heart.

Delighting in the Lord is not a spiritual discipline, but rather an inevitability for those who love God.

March 27

Commit your way to the Lord;
trust in him, and he will act.

Psalm 37:5

I am trusting Thee, Lord Jesus,
    Trusting only Thee!
Trusting thee for full salvation,
    Great and free.
I am trusting Thee to guide me;
    Thou alone shalt lead,
Every day and hour supplying
    All my need.

—Frances R. Havergal,
"I Am Trusting Thee, Lord Jesus"

God is the only proper object of our faith; any
other object is nothing more or less than an idol.

March 28

Be still before the Lord, and wait patiently for him;
do not fret over those who prosper in their way,
over those who carry out evil devices.

Psalm 37:7

Why is it that those who do the right thing so often seem to lose out, while those who take shortcuts and cheat and steal and lie seem to have the advantage? I want to call people on these things—to say something to the person who jumps in front of me in line, to call attention to the lies of that coworker who got away with something he or she shouldn't have, and to set things right when someone isn't being fair! But you call me to be still, Lord—to be still in mind and body—and to wait for you. Please take the grudging attitude from my obedience and help me wait willingly, expectantly, and patiently.

My grandma was witty and wise, and one of the verses she used to remind us of when she knew we were trying to get away with something we shouldn't was "Be sure your sin will find you out" (see Numbers 32:23). "God sees, even if I don't," she told us.

March 29

Refrain from anger, and forsake wrath.
Do not fret—it leads only to evil.

Psalm 37:8

*H*eavenly Father, may I not enter into the kind of consuming anger that eats me up inside. If there is something I'm holding on to— some angry grudge or annoying circumstance I keep mulling over—help me let it go right now, put it into your hands, and walk on, free of its power. In Jesus' name, I pray. Amen.

Be angry, and yet do not sin; do not let the sun go down on your anger, and do not give the devil an opportunity.

—Ephesians 4:26–27 (NASB)

March 30

*M*eekness is amazingly powerful, Lord! In your "economy" everything is upside down from how many people see things. They say that grasping for power and money and fame is the way to make the world your own. You tell me to lay down everything and be humble, and you will bring your power to bear in my life to give me the best kind of spiritual life. Today, I choose your way over the world's.

Meekness sounds a lot like *weakness* and can even *look* like weakness when a person chooses not to take matters into his or her own hands but to wait for God to intercede. Nothing, however, could take more strength of character than that particular act of faith—the act of being gentle, humble, and meek.

March 31

For the Lord loves justice;
he will not forsake his faithful ones.
The righteous shall be kept safe forever.

Psalm 37:28

arm may come knocking at my door, dear Father, but I will not be destroyed by it, because you keep me safe. Darkness may fall on my circumstances, but I will not be lost in it, because you will not forsake me. Evil may seek

me out, but I will not be swallowed up by it, because you come to my aid. Loving Father, you will keep me safe now and forever because I am yours.

If I believe God will keep me safe forever, what can my suffering in this life mean? It can only mean that I am not yet home. But God is faithfully leading me there to my eternal haven, keeping me safe from abandoning the path along the way through this sometimes painful but temporal journey.

April

April 1

*Fools say in their hearts,
"There is no God."*
Psalm 14:1

*L*ord, sometimes it's easy for me to look out at the world and criticize people for godlessness. There's always someone who doesn't measure up. They're fools, aren't they? How can anyone see the glory of creation and *not* want a relationship with the Creator? Are they paying attention at all, or do their selfish desires blind them? That's foolishness! But then I realize that this judgmental spirit is foolish too. Though I believe in you, Lord, I often act as if you don't matter. I often forget all about the love that you have asked for. In such moments, I humbly realize that you love fools, even fools like me.

Though they knew God, they did not honor him as God or give thanks to him, but they became futile in their thinking, and their senseless minds were darkened. Claiming to be wise, they became fools.

—Romans 1:21–22

April 2

Lift up your heads, O gates!
and be lifted up, O ancient doors!
that the King of glory may come in.
Who is the King of glory?
The Lord, strong and mighty,
the Lord, mighty in battle.

Psalm 24:7–8

O victorious Lord, I welcome you into my heart. I cheer with the psalmist, watching the victory parade. You are indeed a conquering king. You have broken the power of sin and death, and now you desire a vibrant relationship with your people. Hail to you, King of glory! I also recall Jesus' triumphal entry, as he rode into Jerusalem not on a warhorse but on a lowly donkey. He intended not to win this victory with a sword but with his own sacrifice. That makes the victory even more glorious. Hail to you, my loving King!

In the ancient world, the victory parade of a conquering king was a spectacular occurrence. We get a meager glimpse of that nowadays when a sports team wins a championship, but the psalmist was pulling out all the stops to welcome the King of Glory.

April 3

Save us, we beseech you, O Lord!
O Lord, we beseech you, give us success!

Psalm 118:25

$\mathcal{I}$t seems as though everyone is grasping for success. In this dog-eat-dog world, there's plenty of pressure to come out on top. Lord, you know that I want success, too—success in the projects I do each day, in my family life, and in my dealings with others. Grant me success, I pray! But then I wonder, *What is success?* And I need to come back to you for the answer. Grant me *true* success, Lord, not the materialistic success the world offers. Let me be truly effective in doing what you want.

The Hebrew words for "Save us, Lord!" from Psalm 118 form the basis of the *Hosanna* shout offered at the triumphal entry of Jesus. It was a cry of praise, but also a call for help directed to someone with the power to help.

April 4

For with you is the fountain of life;
in your light we see light.

Psalm 36:9

ord of life,
I drink from
your fountain. Live
your life through me.
I rejoice in the power
of resurrection and
in the promise of new
life. Because you have
conquered death, we have an eternal existence with
you to anticipate. My soul thrills with this great news.
Let my life radiate with your life. In everything I do,
let me express my love for you, and help me show
your love to others.

All things came into being through him, and
without him not one thing came into being.
What has come into being in him was life,
and the life was the light of all people.

—John 1:3–4

April 5

Sometimes I'm shy, almighty God, when it comes to talking about you. You know how much I treasure the relationship that you and I have, but it's a very personal thing. I don't want to be some know-it-all telling everybody else what to believe. Still, I wish other people would share the joy of this relationship with me. I do want to pass the good news along to other generations of people, but sometimes I lack the courage. So I'm asking you, Lord, for the wisdom to know when to speak, for the love to speak warmly, and for the courage to overcome my fears.

The Easter season is a great opportunity to talk about the Lord in a natural way. It's not really about eggs and bunnies, but about our Savior.

April 6

I come to you humbly, my Lord, well aware of my sins. I have done things to displease you, and I have avoided doing things you wanted me to do. I have not listened to your voice enough. Instead, I often go my own rebellious way. And I bow before you now in sorrow with a broken spirit and a

contrite heart. Please forgive my sins. Jesus sacrificed himself as atonement for my sins, and I claim that sacrifice now. Wipe the record clean and restore our love, I pray.

April 7

Have mercy on me, O God,
according to your steadfast love;
according to your abundant mercy
blot out my transgressions.

Psalm 51:1

Your mercy amazes me, heavenly Father. I am in awe of your capacity to forgive. I know I have disappointed you, and I deserve nothing from you but judgment. Instead, you show mercy to me. You reach out with your steadfast love and welcome me back into your good graces. I thank you for this undeserved favor. I praise you for your overwhelming grace. And I pray for your power to walk in holiness.

For by grace you have been saved through faith, and this is not your own doing; it is the gift of God—not the result of works, so that no one may boast. For we are what he has made us, created in Christ Jesus for good works, which God prepared beforehand to be our way of life.

—Ephesians 2:8–10

April 8

Restore to me the joy of your salvation,
and sustain in me a willing spirit.

Psalm 51:12

I come to you with a tired soul.
My will seems weak; my faith feels old.
I've said the words, the prayers I've prayed;
Good deeds I've done; I've seldom strayed.
My interaction with you, Lord,
Is fine—but now I'm getting bored.
I trust you still for daily bread,
Just lately I've been playing dead.
But wait! Before the break of day
My tombstone slowly rolls away!
The Lord of life stands tall and strong.
I think I hear a victory song.
The risen Christ is raised indeed,
And after that, he raises me.
Salvation's joy has been restored.
Sing praises to our living Lord!

In fact Christ has been raised from the dead,
the first fruits of those who have died.

—1 Corinthians 15:20

April 9

Rain in abundance, O God, you showered abroad;
you restored your heritage when it languished;
your flock found a dwelling in it;
in your goodness, O God, you provided for the needy.

Psalm 68:9–10

*G*reat God, I thank you for the many times you have met my needs—not only material needs but emotional, relational, and spiritual needs as well. Sometimes with near-miracles, but usually in subtler ways, you work your wonders, and I have been blessed. I thank you for the care you've shown to me, and I ask you to help me care for others. Give me eyes to see the needs around me and the strength to do what I can to show your love.

My God will fully satisfy every need of yours according to his riches in glory in Christ Jesus.

—Philippians 4:19

April 10

Teach me your way, O Lord,
and lead me on a level path
because of my enemies.

Psalm 27:11

Dear Lord, because I get tripped up so easily, please stay close beside me. Every step of the way, keep guiding me. When I interact with others  in my daily work, give me a wise head and a caring heart. When I spend time with my family, show me how to serve them best. When I face temptations, show me a way out. I know it's easy to fall; please keep me upright.

God is faithful, and he will not let you be tested beyond your strength, but with the testing he will also provide the way out so that you may be able to endure it.

—1 Corinthians 10:13

April 11

He makes me lie down in green pastures;
he leads me beside still waters;
he restores my soul.
He leads me in right paths
for his name's sake.

Psalm 23:2–3

O Sovereign and almighty Lord, bless all thy people, and all thy flock. Give thy peace, thy help, thy love unto us thy servants, the sheep of thy fold, that we may be united in the bond of peace and love, one body and one spirit, in one hope of our calling, in thy divine and boundless love.

—Liturgy of St. Mark

The thief comes only to steal and kill and destroy. I came that they may have life, and have it abundantly. I am the good shepherd. The good shepherd lays down his life for the sheep.

—John 10:10–11

111

April 12

Blessed is the one who comes in the name of the Lord.
We bless you from the house of the Lord.

Psalm 118:26

Lord Jesus, I remember these words from the psalms that express the praise shouted at your triumphal entry. You rode into Jerusalem on a donkey—a conquering king and a suffering servant. The people welcomed your arrival with glad shouts. In a similar way, I welcome your arrival into my life. Every day, I seek your presence to steer me through my challenges. I need your assurance, your comfort, and your wisdom. So I bless you, dear Lord, with the children of Jerusalem. Thank you for entering my life.

Listen! I am standing at the door, knocking; if you hear my voice and open the door, I will come in to you and eat with you, and you with me.

—Revelation 3:20

April 13

God is our refuge and strength,
a very present help in trouble.
Therefore we will not fear,
though the earth should change.

Psalm 46:1–2

*I*t's hard to keep up with earth's changes, dear Lord. Maybe the psalmist was thinking about storms and seasons, but I'm dealing with technology, social trends, and the environment. Things are spinning so quickly that  I find myself growing fearful at times. But I cling to this promise, and I cling to *you*. You are, indeed, "very present." No matter what's happening in the world, you are with me, beside me, and inside me. I treasure your companionship. Please calm my fears and embolden me to meet the challenges of life with your love and power.

Look for God, and he will find you.

April 14

Singers and dancers alike say,
"All my springs are in you."

Psalm 87:7

Dear Lord, the psalmist spoke about springs of water, and maybe the idea was that the creativity of these artists was springing up from the depths of their relationship with you. That makes me think about the ways I display my own creativity and how it all originates with you. But it's also fun to imagine dancers "springing" and leaping with divine joy. Do I have an extra "spring in my step" because I know you? I also find myself in the season of spring, with new life sprouting all around me. Every day with you is like springtime, full of life and growth. Lord, in these ways I celebrate you, singing with the psalmist, "All my springs are in you."

Those who drink of the water that I will give them will never be thirsty. The water that I will give will become in them a spring of water gushing up to eternal life.

—John 4:14

April 15

*Better is a little that the righteous person has
than the abundance of many wicked.*

Psalm 37:16

Everyone's talking about the tax deadline, Lord, and I'm hearing a lot of gripes. People are feeling poor as they count up their earnings and figure out what they owe. But I want to focus today on my true wealth. This can't be measured in dollars and cents but rather in love and grace. You, Lord, have showered abundant blessings upon me. Just to know you is a great reward, and I am grateful. There are many people in this world who are rolling in dough but are far from you. You keep reminding me that I am better off than they are. Thank you, Lord.

There is great gain in godliness combined with contentment. . . . But those who want to be rich fall into temptation and are trapped by many senseless and harmful desires that plunge people into ruin and destruction. For the love of money is a root of all kinds of evil.

—1 Timothy 6:6, 9–10

April 16

Open to me the gates of righteousness,
that I may enter through them
and give thanks to the Lord.

Psalm 118:19

Glorious Lord, I come before you to worship. I don't take this privilege lightly. I imagine the ancient Israelites climbing the steep streets of Jerusalem toward the Temple and entering through those beautiful gates. I imagine the priests entering the Holy Place with the sacred incense and holy bread, and the high priest venturing into the Holy of Holies. Coming into your presence is a sacred trust. But I don't have to climb a hill; I can kneel in my home. You have already opened the gates to your presence, and you invite me to enter whenever I will. So, here I am to worship. You are my great God. I thank you, and I love you.

Therefore, I urge you, brothers, in view of God's mercy, to offer your bodies as living sacrifices, holy and pleasing to God—this is your spiritual act of worship.

—Romans 12:1 (NIV)

April 17

Happy are the people who know the festal shout,
who walk, O Lord, in the light of your countenance;
they exult in your name all day long,
and extol your righteousness.

Psalm 89:15–16

God of joy, you fill my heart with good things. You bestow your loving smile upon me and satisfy my longings. Life is full of blessings when I live each day in your presence. Thank you for the joy you bring to me. Help me share that joy with others.

Jesus told several stories about banquets and was a regular guest at dinner parties, much to the chagrin of his critics. Yet even the Old Testament is full of such celebrations. The psalmist's "festal shout" is the happy cry of people celebrating the Lord's goodness.

April 18

O sing to the Lord a new song,
for he has done marvelous things.
His right hand and his holy arm
have gotten him victory.

Psalm 98:1

My Lord, I can't begin to count the marvelous things you have done in my life. I look back through the blessings you have provided—timely help, important relationships, and wise guidance.  There were tough times that prepared me for later challenges. There were joyous surprises that lifted my spirit. Through it all, you have taken good care of me, and I appreciate it. Let my life be a "new song" dedicated to you.

Sing not lolling at ease or in the indecent posture of sitting, drawling out one word after another, but all standing before God, and praising him lustily, and with good courage.

—John Wesley

April 19

For he will command his angels concerning you
to guard you in all your ways.
On their hands they will bear you up,
so that you will not dash your foot against a stone.

Psalm 91:11–12

I don't know much about angels, Lord,
But I'm really glad they're around
Rendering timely help.
I don't think I've ever seen one, Lord,
Which is just as well, because they'd
Surely scare me silly.
I don't want to worship angels, Lord,
Because they are all just
Servants like me.
But thank you for their help, Lord.

The tempter quoted Scripture to Jesus, trying to persuade him to jump off the Temple roof. Jesus replied with another verse, forbidding the testing of God. Don't be foolhardy about playing with danger, just because you trust God to rescue you.

April 20

They are like trees
planted by streams of water,
which yield their fruit in its season,
and their leaves do not wither.
In all that they do, they prosper.

Psalm 1:3

Nourishing Lord, I want to grow in you. Let me drink in your goodness and bear spiritual fruit. This is what I was made for, isn't it? To thrive in an ongoing relationship with you? Speak to me as I come before you each day, not only praying but also listening. Instruct me as I read your Word. Guide me as I live each moment. Use other believers to encourage me and steer me in the right direction. Empower me to touch others with your love. I may be just a sapling now, Lord, but I'm growing— with your help.

The glory of God is a person fully alive.

—Irenaeus

April 21

You prepare a table before me
in the presence of my enemies;
you anoint my head with oil;
my cup overflows.

Psalm 23:5

As I read these familiar words from David's cherished psalm, Lord Jesus, I reflect on the Last Supper, where you did "prepare a table" before your disciples. I also know that although you were about to meet your enemies, you celebrated this moment with your disciples, sharing your wisdom, your new instructions, and *yourself* with them. The bread and wine took on a whole new meaning, which we still observe today. Lord, thank you for the gift of yourself—shared with your disciples then and always at that table and wherever we now meet to partake of you.

For where two or three are gathered in
my name, I am there among them.

—Matthew 18:20

April 22

Into your hand I commit my spirit;
you have redeemed me, O Lord, faithful God.

Psalm 31:5

This was your death-cry from the cross, Lord Jesus. You were suffering for our sins, yet you forgave your tormentors. You felt forsaken by your Father, yet you committed yourself to him in those last moments. This serves as a great example for me, not just as a way to meet death but as a way to greet life. How would my life change if I began each day committing my spirit into the hand of my Creator God? Thank you, Lord, for redeeming me and for showing me how to live.

To say we're "in good hands" when we commit ourselves to God is the supreme understatement. He has the whole world in his hands. By committing ourselves, we're simply acknowledging that fact.

April 23

Then I acknowledged my sin to you,
and I did not hide my iniquity;
I said, "I will confess my transgressions to the Lord,"
and you forgave the guilt of my sin.

Psalm 32:5

I am a sinner. You and I both know that, Lord. There are all sorts of self-help books that wouldn't want me to say that. I'm "misunderstood" or "guilt-afflicted" or "not living up to my potential." But the simple truth is this: I've done wrong. In my thoughts and deeds, in my actions and attitudes toward others, toward myself, and toward you, I have disobeyed you, and I'm sorry. But the story doesn't end there. You offer forgiveness for my sins, no matter how heinous they are. You restore my relationship with you. You wipe the slate clean. Thank you, beloved Lord. I bless you from the depths of my renewed heart.

To err is human, to forgive divine.

—Alexander Pope

123

April 24

For you have delivered my soul from death,
and my feet from falling,
so that I may walk before God
in the light of life.

Psalm 56:13

Now let the angelic choir in the heavens
 rejoice,
Let the divine mysteries be celebrated,
And let a sacred trumpet proclaim the victory of
 such a great King.
Let the earth also be filled with joy, illuminated with
 such resplendent rays;
And let everyone know that the darkness which
 overspread the whole world
Is chased away by the splendor of our eternal King.

—"Exsultet," an ancient Christian prayer

So if you have been raised with Christ, seek the
things that are above, where Christ is,
seated at the right hand of God.

—Colossians 3:1

April 25

He covers the heavens with clouds,
prepares rain for the earth,
makes grass grow on the hills.

Psalm 147:8

My Creator, the more I know about creation, the more I want to praise you. You have made a universe that flows together in a beautiful way. The sun heats the earth, creating water vapor that forms clouds and returns to earth in the form of rain, which makes the grass grow, which feeds animals, and so on. It is a beautiful pattern—one that reflects your wisdom, power, and love. I hope I never again complain about the rain, because it's all part of the intricate design you have put in place.

Ever since the creation of the world his eternal power and divine nature, invisible though they are, have been understood and seen through the things he has made.

—Romans 1:20

April 26

Because your steadfast love is better than life,
my lips will praise you.
So I will bless you as long as I live;
I will lift up my hands and call on your name.

Psalm 63:3–4

*D*ear Lord, you know I have choices all the time—what to do, what to say, how to spend my time, and where to spend my money. Sometimes I have to choose between good and bad, but often the options are what's good and what's better. I have to agree with the psalmist that your love is better than life itself. Everything that I would choose to improve my life, to get ahead in life, and to make my life more comfortable or successful or exciting—it all pales in importance when compared to my relationship with you. That's why I praise you, bless you, and rely on you for all I need. Blessed be the name of the Lord.

The Hebrew word translated "steadfast love" here and throughout the Old Testament (more than 200 times) is *chesed.* Two ideas collide in this word—strength and compassion. It's a deep-felt expression of fierce loyalty. It's a kindness that the person doesn't have to show but wants to.

April 27

I am like a green olive tree
in the house of God.
I trust in the steadfast love of God
forever and ever.

Psalm 52:8

I've seen trees, Lord of the universe, that are thick with age, standing tall and strong. Birds nest in their branches. Perhaps children climb on them. These trees provide shelter from the rain and shade from the sun. They beautify the landscape. In all these ways, they provide joy and benefit to everyone in the vicinity. I want to be like that, too. Sometimes I feel like merely a twig, but I want to grow strong in you. Build me up, make me strong, and let me be a blessing to everyone around me.

I pray that, according to the riches of his glory, he may grant that you may be strengthened in your inner being with power through his Spirit, and that Christ may dwell in your hearts through faith, as you are being rooted and grounded in love.

—Ephesians 3:16–17

April 28

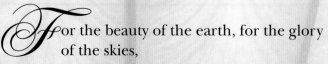

From your lofty abode you water the mountains;
the earth is satisfied with the fruit of your work.

Psalm 104:13

For the beauty of the earth, for the glory
    of the skies,
For the love which from our birth over and around
    us lies,
Lord of all, to thee we raise this our hymn of
    grateful praise. . . .

For thyself, best gift divine, to the world so freely
    given,
For that great, great love of thine, peace on earth,
    and joy in heaven,
Lord of all, to thee we raise this our hymn of
    grateful praise.

—Folliot S. Pierpoint

As for those who in the present age are rich,
command them not to be haughty, or to set
their hopes on the uncertainty of riches,
but rather on God who richly provides us
with everything for our enjoyment.

—1 Timothy 6:17

April 29

ear God, I'm learning that life is better when I follow your lead. It might not always seem as if that's true. Sometimes I try to test out my own plans, but invariably it becomes apparent that you know  better. I'm learning to seek your will from the start and not as an afterthought. In all sorts of situations, I'm learning to question my own (frequently selfish) motives and to consider what you want. Please be patient with me. I'm learning slowly, but I *am* learning.

Our wills are ours, we know not how;
Our wills are ours, to make them Thine.

—Alfred Tennyson, "In Memoriam"

April 30

I will bless the Lord at all times;
his praise shall continually be in my mouth.

Psalm 34:1

Praise to the Lord, the Almighty, the King
    of creation!
O my soul, praise him, for he is thy health and salvation!
All ye who hear, now to his temple draw near;
Join me in glad adoration! . . .

Praise to the Lord! O let all that is in me adore him!
All that hath life and breath, come now with praises
    before him!
Let the amen sound from his temple again;
Gladly forever adore him.

—Joachim Neander

The whole multitude of the disciples began to
praise God joyfully with a loud voice for all
the deeds of power that they had seen.

—Luke 19:37

May

May 1

The heavens are telling the glory of God;
and the firmament proclaims his handiwork.

Psalm 19:1

*A*s the changes of spring break out, my Lord (even the rains from the firmament), they shout that you exist, that you are the Creator, and that you are glorious! I revel in this onset of new life and loveliness. May I, too, be a faithful witness of who you are and what you're like.

As beautiful and wondrous as nature is, with its towering mountains, gorgeous meadows, lush forests, mighty rivers, and magnificent animal life, it is not God. Rather, nature is the work of the Creator, and as such, it reveals how truly awesome is our God, who created us as well.

May 2

I waited patiently for the Lord;
he inclined to me and heard my cry.

Psalm 40:1

*P*recious Lord, your Word reveals that patience is the fruit of a life lived in step with your Holy Spirit. Therefore, I ask that, instead of my trying to be patient through self-effort or beating myself up for my lack of patience, you would help me focus on being led by your Spirit in all circumstances, allowing your Spirit to guide me, speak into my life, and live through me at each juncture where patience is required. As I focus on following your lead, I know my life will begin to bear that good fruit of patient waiting and living.

But the fruit of the Spirit is love, joy, peace, patience, kindness, goodness, faithfulness, gentleness, self-control; against such things there is no law.

—Galatians 5:22–23 (NASB)

133

May 3

I have not hidden your saving help within my heart,
I have spoken of your faithfulness and your salvation;
I have not concealed your steadfast love and your faithfulness.

Psalm 40:10

Dear Lord, when I sense that you are opening an opportunity for me to talk to someone about you—whether it's a word about your saving grace, your faithfulness, or your constant love—help me to not be afraid to speak up. Help me treat those to whom I'm speaking with gentleness and respect as I dialogue about faith in you. And for those who are looking for you, may my words help them find you.

We can enjoy talking about our faith if we relax and simply tell our own story of how God has loved us so deeply and devotedly.

May 4

*But may all who seek you
rejoice and be glad in you;
may those who love your salvation
say continually, "Great is the Lord!"*

Psalm 40:16

Heavenly Father,
you *are* great!
I am truly grateful for your
salvation, and as I continually
seek you, I rejoice in
everything you reveal to me
about yourself. I am, indeed,
glad in you today. I feel
blessed and deeply honored
to be here with you, the God
of the universe. When I try to think about it, it's a
reality that's hard to wrap my mind around, and
yet it's true. May I continually be in awe of your
greatness and be full of delight when I reflect on
who you are and how you have saved me.

If God's greatness is powerfully evident to us,
we can imagine those around his throne
in heaven continually worshipping him.

May 5

Happy are those who consider the poor;
the Lord delivers them in the day of trouble.

Psalm 41:1

*Y*ou have told us, great Lord,
to love our neighbors as
ourselves, to do unto others as we'd
have them do to us. You have also
said that I will reap what I sow in
this life. So help me, loving Father, to
remember the poor—whether they are
poor in finances, abilities, social graces, health, or
any other kind of poverty. Show me how you would
minister to them. Remind me of how Jesus walked
and talked and ministered to those in need, and by
your Spirit, lead me in doing as Jesus has done. For
the honor of your name, I pray. Amen.

The purpose of life is to listen—to yourself, to
your neighbor, to your world, and to God—and,
when the time comes, to respond in as helpful a
way as you can find...from within and without.

—Fred Rogers, *The World According to Mister Rogers:*
Important Things to Remember

136

May 6

By day the Lord commands his steadfast love,
and at night his song is with me,
a prayer to the God of my life.

Psalm 42:8

Come, Thou Fount of every blessing,
Tune my heart to sing Thy grace;
Streams of mercy never ceasing,
Call for songs of loudest praise.
Teach me some melodious sonnet,
Sung by flaming tongues above.
Praise the mount—I'm fixed upon it—
Mount of Thy redeeming love.

—Robert Robinson, "Come, Thou Fount"

What song of praise can I sing to my Lord
and Savior right now that I can carry in
my heart and on my lips throughout
the day and into the night, and
even as I drift off to sleep?

May 7

We have heard with our ears, O God,
our ancestors have told us,
what deeds you performed in their days,
in the days of old.

Psalm 44:1

Almighty Father, help me be faithful to tell the younger generation about you. Help me not assume either that they know or that they don't really care to hear about spiritual realities. Remind me of the stories of good things you have done in my life when I'm around children, and even teens. Then, I pray that you would grant me a gift of articulation so that I can communicate in ways that reach their inner being and stir up a longing to know you. May there always be people in each successive generation who love to sing your praise.

We're on a "pay it forward" plan when it comes to the gospel. Each successive generation has passed on the Good News to the next. We now have the privilege of "paying it forward" to those who will come after us.

May 8

Be still, and know that I am God!
I am exalted among the nations,
I am exalted in the earth.

Psalm 46:10

At times when stillness is not part of my outer world, Lord, I need more than ever to answer your call to quiet my heart and mind before you. I thank you that when I do stop to regain perspective, remembering that you are God, everything else finds its proper place in light of who you are. I have come to be still right now and to exalt you as God in my life. I thank you that I can place myself under your sovereignty and find peace in your safety, provision, and love.

Solitude is the place where we can find quality one-on-one time with God. Even when life is busy, we can lay hold of opportunities for brief times of solitude whether we're driving, showering, exercising, or doing yard work—anything that allows us to be alone for a little while.

May 9

We ponder your steadfast love, O God,
in the midst of your temple.

Psalm 48:9

Your Word reminds me that my body is the temple of your Holy Spirit and that you dwell within me. It is from within this "temple," dear Lord, that I find myself thinking about your love. I remember how you have revealed your love for me time and again in the many ways you have cared for me. You are my provision with your healing, protection, salvation, comfort, peace, forgiveness, kindness, goodness, gentleness, and faithfulness. There are so many ways you have made it clear to me that you love me. As I continue pondering your great love, make me aware of how I can show that love to those around me.

Love is simply an idea until it is put into action; we can say "I love you" as many times as we'd like, but until we act in love, our words are just sounds, clanging cymbals (read 1 Corinthians 13).

140

May 10

Your name, O God, like your praise,
reaches to the ends of the earth.

Psalm 48:10

May you be praised wherever you are and recognized for who you are, Lord God! May my praise from this "end of the earth" rise up to meet the praises of those around the world. We give you glory and honor this day for all you have done

in the past to bring about our salvation, for all you are doing even now to save others, and for all you will do to bring every promise you have made to fulfillment. In Jesus' name, I pray. Amen.

Now unto the King eternal, immortal, invisible, the only wise God, be honour and glory for ever and ever. Amen.

—1 Timothy 1:17 (KJV)

May 11

For every wild animal of the forest is mine,
the cattle on a thousand hills.
I know all the birds of the air,
and all that moves in the field is mine.

Psalm 50:10–11

Although you have entrusted humanity with the care of your creation, heavenly Father, all of it still belongs to you. Remind me to be a good caretaker of all that you have entrusted to me in my corner of the world. Grant me your wisdom as I make choices about how to best tend those things in my care. Help me be diligent to do what is within my power to be a responsible tenant while I'm here. Bless and multiply the efforts of those who are doing good and honest work to care for your creation.

If your heart is straight with God, then every creature will be to you a mirror of life and a book of holy doctrine. No creature is so little or so mean as not to show forth and represent the goodness of God.

—Thomas à Kempis, *The Imitation of Christ*

May 12

You desire truth in the inward being;
therefore teach me wisdom in my secret heart.

Psalm 51:6

It's easy to put on a "face" for the world, Lord, but the only face I can come to you with is my own. What is true about me even escapes my realization sometimes, until I enter your presence and drop all of my self-notions and wait for you to reveal the truth to me. Sometimes it's not easy to accept what you show me; sometimes I feel ashamed when I become aware of the pride and pretension I've used to get by in my relationships with others. But you lead me quickly out of shame and into your forgiveness, truth, and love, and that is where I find the depth of fellowship with you that I crave.

Truth may hurt initially when we learn it, just as a needle piercing an infected wound. But after all of the pent-up lies, pride, and pretense have been let out, there is a wonderful feeling of relief and freedom that quickly follows as we embrace the cleansing of God's loving truth.

May 13

Create in me a clean heart, O God,
and put a new and right spirit within me.

Psalm 51:10

Every sojourn outside of this sanctuary of your presence brings me back to this prayer, gracious Father. As I come to you, I sense your holiness and can feel my need to be made clean again. Please wash me with your Word, and renew me by your Spirit. Recalibrate my conscience so that it is in line with your desires for me once again. In Jesus' name, I pray. Amen.

A tender conscience is a spiritual safeguard and should never be ignored or despised.

May 14

O Lord, open my lips,
and my mouth will declare your praise.

Psalm 51:15

Sometimes I just don't feel like praising you, heavenly Father, even though I know you deserve my praise 24/7. When my tongue seems stuck to the roof of my mouth and when my soul meets the idea of rejoicing with a grumpy attitude, please trump my temporary funk. Wash over

my sour soul with a fresh awareness of your greatness and goodness. Open my mouth by opening my heart and filling it with sincere praise once again.

Sometimes it takes an act of our will to override uncooperative emotions and give God the praise he deserves.

May 15

I have calmed and quieted my soul,
like a child quieted at its mother's breast;
like a child that is quieted is my soul.

Psalm 131:2 (RSV)

Holding other people's babies is a treat, heavenly Father, but it's an almost universal reality that a baby is never truly at peace and rest until it is returned to its mother's arms. It's like that with your children. We venture out into the world and go about our business, as if we are handed around from this set of arms to another. It isn't until we can return to your presence—the resting place of our souls—that we feel like a child at its mother's breast—quieted, calmed, and able to truly rest.

If my soul is disquieted, restless, frustrated, and "fussy," perhaps it is time for me to be quieted in the arms of my God.

May 16

But surely, God is my helper;
the Lord is the upholder of my life.

Psalm 54:4

When things go wrong in my life, dear Lord, help me live out this declaration. May I entrust to you all that pertains to my life, even my life itself: from broken appliances to broken bones and to broken promises—every form of fragmentation, frustration, and pain that life in this fallen world can dish out. May I seek and know you as my helper, the upholder of my life.

We count our blessings when we praise God. If we count our problems, let it be in order that we may, in faith, call on God as our helper.

May 17

Cast your burden on the Lord,
and he will sustain you;
he will never permit
the righteous to be moved.

Psalm 55:22

When I try to carry my burdens on my own, Lord, the weight of them eventually crushes me. In time, I become

incapacitated while I stumble along—pride-driven, stubborn, and thinking I should be able to do this or that. How much easier and how much better for me to unburden my heart, mind, soul, and strength to you, lifting my pack of problems from my shoulders and casting them onto yours!

I cannot know God's sustaining grace until I put an end to my self-sustaining ways.

May 18

When I am afraid,
I put my trust in you.
In God, whose word I praise,
in God I trust; I am not afraid;
what can flesh do to me?

Psalm 56:3–4

Many times I have found, Lord God, that your Word has shored up my faith when circumstances have shaken me to the core. Fear, anxiety, uncertainty, and worry all disappear like morning mists when the light of your truth begins its ascent above the horizon of my mind and warms my panic-chilled heart. I praise you for your Word, which is able to empower my faith, to rally hope within my soul, and to muster the cry of victory because of your great and precious promises. I fear only you because I trust in you alone.

What promise in God's Word speaks peace to your situation today? Begin by reading Philippians 4:6–7. It is a good place to start.

May 19

I cry to God Most High,
to God who fulfills his purpose for me.

Psalm 57:2

You know all the purposes for which you have made me, Lord God: to fellowship with you; to enjoy meaningful relationships with others; to declare your praises, to minister to those in need . . . the list is long. But I'm so grateful that I don't need to make a purpose-fulfillment to-do list for myself. You are the one who fulfills your purpose for those who love you. So I cry out to you today to increase my love for you that I might more readily lay down my own agenda to be available to fulfill the excellent purposes you have for me.

When we focus on being love-driven, God takes care of the purpose-driven aspect of our lives.

May 20

My heart is steadfast, O God,
my heart is steadfast.
I will sing and make melody.
Awake, my soul!

Psalm 57:7–8

The prayer for the New Year in this book was a commitment to seek to be glad in you and to let that gladness overflow into song. I pray now for a renewed steadfastness of heart that will continue to pursue the practice of praise. Let today be a day of song, of singing your praises because you are faithful and good to me.

If you look around you and find only reasons to rejoice today, praise God for his goodness, for he is the source of every good gift. But if you look around and find only reasons to be upset today, praise God for his faithfulness, for he is upholding you in the midst of your trials.

151

May 21

Deliver me from my enemies, O my God;
protect me from those who rise up against me.

Psalm 59:1

When my enemies rise up against me, almighty Father, I'm tempted to ask you to crush and destroy them. But I pray that you would fill my heart with mercy so that, instead of asking for revenge, I will merely ask with the psalmist that you will rescue and protect me from those who seek to harm me. I'll leave with you the weighty matter of judgment and be free of that burden. Meanwhile, I do ask that you would not allow my enemies to have their way with my life, for I belong to you.

The path of mercy and forgiveness may be excruciating at times, but the alternative path of bitterness and revenge is spiritually fatal.

May 22

Hear my cry, O God;
listen to my prayer.
From the end of the earth I call to you,
when my heart is faint.
Lead me to the rock
that is higher than I.

Psalm 61:1–2

Heavenly Father, help me approach you from a place of humility, where I can see how magnificent and strong you are—a towering rock and a powerful presence. Then my faint heart will be encouraged, and my faith will find its rightful object. When my heart is overcome, may it be comforted when it looks up to you and helped when it calls upon you.

The Grand Canyon is an awe-inspiring place, but the lesser-known Zion National Park is, in the opinion of many, an even more powerful experience. From the rims of the Grand Canyon, one stands above the vast folds and layers and pillars of rock, looking down upon them. From within Zion, however, one enters its canyons from below and is always looking up at the towering rock features. It's an entirely different perspective.

153

May 23

He alone is my rock and my salvation,
my fortress; I shall not be shaken.

Psalm 62:6

D ear Father, please reveal truth to me. Do I have other crumbly rocks or false fortresses I look to for help, protection, or comfort? Do I look to them first and then to you as a last

resort? I don't want this kind of arrangement in my life anymore. Please lead me away from them; show me how fragile and shakable they are. You are my rock that cannot be shaken. I need only you!

Where we find addiction in our lives is a good indicator of false fortresses and crumbling rocks we've set up as a form of "salvation." Seek God for a path out of addiction, whether it be to television, food, sex, alcohol, drugs, work, shopping—anything we turn to compulsively for comfort and help.

154

May 24

Trust in him at all times, O people;
pour out your heart before him.

Psalm 62:8

All-powerful Lord, sometimes my prayer life seems like a list of needs or a litany of superficial thoughts. My heart isn't always in it. And when I think about how a human relationship would fare if there was just cognitive communication with no heart-level interaction, I see my deep need to engage my heart in our relationship. Help me as I seek to open up to you more and more in the days ahead.

Ruts in our prayer life can occur when we're bringing our thoughts to God on a regular basis without the accompanying powerful passions of the heart. To pour out our heart in prayer is to tell God our deepest desires, to let him in on our fears and hurts and frustrations, and to invite him to join us where we really live.

May 25

My soul clings to you;
your right hand upholds me.

Psalm 63:8

Like a burr to wool, like plastic wrap to a glass bowl, like a static electricity–charged sock to polyester, like a fullback to the football, like road tar to my car's fender…may I cling tenaciously to you, O Lord. And may I feel your presence as I hold fast to you. How I always need you!

As a biblical metaphor, a right hand represents strength and the place of favor or honor. Today's verse indicates that it is God's right hand that upholds us. We find ourselves, then, the beneficiaries of both his strength and his favor.

May 26

All the earth worships you;
they sing praises to you,
sing praises to your name.

Psalm 66:4

May I hear the songs of praise around me, great Lord, as I, too, seek to worship you in song. The songbirds, geese, flowing waters, ocean waves, falling rain, thunderstorms, rustling leaves, frogs, crickets, coyotes, wolves... so much of nature sings, and to me it sounds as if praise and thanks are being lifted to you. It sounds as if your creation is reveling in your goodness. Today I'll join my voice to theirs, and together we will worship you.

What music can you hear right now as you listen, whether it be music from within or from without? Use it as a springboard for your own worship right now!

May 27

*May God be gracious to us and bless us
and make his face to shine upon us.*

Psalm 67:1

When your blessings flow into my life, dear Lord, it certainly feels like situational sunshine, as if you are looking upon my life with a megawatt smile. Help me remember your blessings and recount them often so that I do not forget that I have been and always am sustained solely by your grace. In Jesus' name, I pray. Amen.

The Lord bless you and keep you; the Lord make his face shine upon you, and be gracious to you; the Lord lift up his countenance upon you, and give you peace.

—Numbers 6:24–26

May 28

*Blessed be the Lord,
who daily bears us up;
God is our salvation.*

Psalm 68:19

When I read this verse, dear Lord, I think of a father scooping up his daughter to carry her in his arms or on his shoulders. I think of the delight on the child's face as she is raised to that place of security and fellowship. I see the relaxed form of the child as she leans into the father's strong frame. I see the way the two of them sway in sync with the father's gait. I hear their conversation, unhindered and on the child's level of understanding. This is how you are with your children, heavenly Father. This is how you bear us up each day. My trust belongs to you.

In humanity, there are good fathers and ones who have failed miserably. If a person has had the latter kind of father, it helps to find a good father figure to watch in action to repair a broken understanding of what being a good father means.

159

May 29

O God, you know my folly;
the wrongs I have done are not hidden from you.

Psalm 69:5

O Father! If only I could undo my foolish decisions. There is much I have done—or failed to do—that I would change. But these are irretrievable realities, and yet, they are not unredeemable. Each wrong  that I bring to you and confess, you readily forgive and begin the process of redemption, of bringing some good out of the aftermath of my downfall. I'm deeply grateful for these miracles, but I pray that you would cause me to grow wiser from my mistakes and more faithful so I can walk in your righteousness.

Regrets are often the fruit of our foolishness, and yet redemption is the fruit of God's forgiveness for each regretful choice.

May 30

For the Lord hears the needy,
and does not despise his own that are in bonds.

Psalm 69:33

O Lord, I'm trapped! I've gotten myself in a situation I cannot get out of. This bondage is suffocating, and I feel panicked. I didn't listen to you, and now it's too late to heed

the wisdom of your counsel. Please forgive me and rescue me. Even as I pray, there is a fear that you will turn away and say that you told me so. And you would be justified in doing that, Lord. But please don't despise me. Have mercy on me! In Jesus' name, I pray. Amen.

God's goal is not to punish but to teach—
not to shame but to save.

May 31

Rescue me, O my God, from the hand of the wicked,
from the grasp of the unjust and cruel.

Psalm 71:4

*J*esus, you know what it is to be lied about, unjustly condemned, and cruelly tortured and killed at the hands of wicked people. I ask that you would hear my cry for help to be set free from the evil schemes of those who would try to harm me without cause. I look to you alone for my defense. Please rescue me! In your name, I pray. Amen.

One of my wise teachers, Dr. William F. Orr, told me, "There is only one thing evil cannot stand and that is forgiveness."

—Fred Rogers, *The World According to Mister Rogers:*
Important Things to Remember

June

June 1

You, O Lord, are a shield around me,
my glory, and the one who lifts up my head.

Psalm 3:3

Dear Lord, I thank you for these three wonderful things you do for me. First, you shield me from harm. That's not to say that I'm immune from the ups and downs of life, but you keep the downs from destroying me. And I shudder to think what my life would be like without you. Second, you provide "glory"—not that I get to glorify myself, but through you I connect with your amazing and eternal resplendence. Finally, you "lift up my head." When I'm in the doldrums, you come to me with exceeding joy. Thank you for these remarkable gifts.

I consider that the sufferings of this present time are not worth comparing with the glory about to be revealed to us.

—Romans 8:18

June 2

Let them praise his name with dancing,
making melody to him with tambourine and lyre.
For the Lord takes pleasure in his people...
let them sing for joy on their couches.

Psalm 149:3–5

*S*ometimes, my Lord, you make me feel like dancing; other times I'm just as happy to rest on the couch. In both situations, I celebrate your presence and your pleasure. I exult in the life you have given me. You created this body of mine, and I'm delighted to use it to praise you. But when this body gets weary, I can still enjoy you in the stillness. It fills me with joy to think that I can give you pleasure. Be pleased, dear Lord, with my life.

Some scholars think that the psalmist's word for "couch" really refers to a mat used for kneeling, so these "couches" are dedicated places of worship. That makes sense, and it raises the question: What are we worshiping when we're on *our* couches?

165

June 3

I can look at a sunset and marvel at your handiwork. You are the consummate artist, marvelous Lord, swirling cloud colors in ever-new designs. I can look at a mountain standing proud or an ocean pounding onto the shore, and I brim with wonder at your awesome creativity. But then I notice I can get a much closer view of your artistry any time I want it. You have created *me*. My body and mind contain intricate patterns wonderful to behold, and you created my spirit to commune with yours. Lord, I thrill to think of all you have made, including myself.

June 4

Unless the Lord builds the house,
those who build it labor in vain.
Unless the Lord guards the city,
the guard keeps watch in vain.

Psalm 127:1

Build my life, supreme Lord, and keep watch over it. You know I have often tried to build my life in my own way. I have made my own choices about relationships, school, work, activities, and so on. Sometimes you have seen  fit to bless my decisions, but other times I just find that these parts of my life are empty, pointless, and unsatisfying. So let me now turn over the building process to you, my Lord. Guide me in all my life decisions and guard my heart.

For we are God's servants, working together; you are God's field, God's building.

—1 Corinthians 3:9

167

June 5

Let those who are wise give heed to these things,
and consider the steadfast love of the Lord.

Psalm 107:43

*I*t's cap-and-gown time again, Lord God. At high schools and colleges all over this land, people are graduating from their courses of study. It is assumed that they have gathered enough knowledge to move on to the next challenges of life—and hopefully they've even picked up some wisdom along the way. Now you remind me, Lord, that wisdom starts with you. No matter what sort of degrees I might have, if I don't understand that your love is at the heart of all existence, then I'm missing the point. I want to carry that knowledge with me every day, and I want to teach it to others. I want this wisdom to infuse every aspect of my life.

Those who are wise understand these things;
those who are discerning know them.
For the ways of the Lord are right,
and the upright walk in them, but
transgressors stumble in them.

—Hosea 14:9

June 6

*[God] satisfies you with good as long as you live
so that your youth is renewed like the eagle's.*

Psalm 103:5

rise today
   Through the strength of heaven,
   Light of sun,
   Radiance of moon,
   Splendor of fire,
   Speed of lightning,
   Swiftness of wind,
   Depth of sea,
   Stability of earth,
   Firmness of rock.

—early Scottish prayer

Even youths will faint and be weary,
and the young will fall exhausted;
but those who wait for the Lord
shall renew their strength, they shall
mount up with wings like eagles,
they shall run and not be weary,
they shall walk and not faint.

—Isaiah 40:30–31

June 7

Happy are those whom you discipline, O Lord,
and whom you teach out of your law.

Psalm 94:12

I've never liked discipline much, heavenly Father. It makes me think of childhood punishments—being grounded, going to bed without dessert, that sort of thing. But apparently your discipline should make me "happy." How can that be? Well, I suppose I could refer to a marine who has gone through boot camp and is now ready for anything, or a musician who has spent hours practicing and now can touch the angels with a song, or a student who begins with Cs and Ds but ends up graduating with honors. Sometimes I've wondered why the life of faith is excruciatingly difficult, Lord, but I'm beginning to see that you're teaching me through it all—and that makes me truly happy.

No pain, no palm; no thorns, no throne;
no gall, no glory; no cross, no crown.

—William Penn

June 8

I would feed you with the finest of the wheat,
and with honey from the rock I would satisfy you.

Psalm 81:16

I thank you, dear Lord, for your daily provision. You provide me with the income I need to meet life's basic needs, but you also provide companionship, mental stimulation, and spiritual challenge. Day by day, you sustain my life. Once in a while you surprise me with some unexpected blessing. The psalmist talks about "honey from the rock," and honestly the last thing I expect from my rocky existence is sweetness. But you pull a kind word out of a sworn enemy, a new talent out of a hopeless struggle, and a good friend out of a crisis. I have learned to trust you for what I need each day, but please keep surprising me with these extra blessings. They make life with you a delight.

My child, eat honey, for it is good,
and the drippings of the honeycomb
are sweet to your taste.

—Proverbs 24:13

171

June 9

O Lord, you have searched me and known me.
You know when I sit down and when I rise up;
you discern my thoughts from far away.

Psalm 139:1–2

I know you see right through me.
It's sometimes terrifying
How honestly you view me.
But then I think, how awesome
That you completely "get" me.
Despite my sins and problems
You don't want to reject me.
No scowling, Lord, no scolding
In your thorough knowledge of me.
The wonder that's unfolding
Is the fact that you still love me.

For now we see in a mirror, dimly,
but then we will see face to face.
Now I know only in part; then
I will know fully, even as I
have been fully known.

—1 Corinthians 13:12

June 10

Happy are those whom you choose and bring near
to live in your courts.
We shall be satisfied with the goodness of your house,
your holy temple.

Psalm 65:4

My Lord, I thank you for those people who have devoted their lives to ministry: preachers and teachers and nursery workers, administrators and musicians and janitors. Their unselfish service has truly enriched my life, and I know you are ultimately the source of their service, having inspired them to do what they do. Today I pray for them. Empower them to do their work with joy and efficiency. Help them get past all fatigue and discouragement to keep at it. Continue to awaken your love within them for the people they serve.

Do you not know that you are God's temple
and that God's Spirit dwells in you?

—1 Corinthians 3:16

June 11

Why should I fear in times of trouble,
when the iniquity of my persecutors surrounds me,
those who trust in their wealth
and boast of the abundance of their riches?

Psalm 49:5–6

*H*ow easily I get swept into the love of money! Lord, I know that you are all I need. I'd rather have you than all the wealth on earth, but lately I've been worrying about financial matters. All over the news media, I hear the voices of those who trust in their riches, and I'm tempted to join them, to want more, and to fear having less. But then I hear your gentle wooing. You are truly enough for me, dear Lord. I need not fret. I can trust you to provide.

Therefore I tell you, do not worry about your life, what you will eat or what you will drink, or about your body, what you will wear. Is not life more than food, and the body more than clothing? . . . But strive first for the kingdom of God and his righteousness, and all these things will be given to you as well.

—Matthew 6:25, 33

June 12

Have mercy on me, O God,
according to your steadfast love;
according to your abundant mercy
blot out my transgressions.

Psalm 51:1

Depth of mercy! Can there be
Mercy still reserved for me?
Can my God his wrath forbear,
Me, the chief of sinners, spare?
I have long withstood his grace,
Long provoked him to his face,
Would not hearken to his calls,
Grieved him by a thousand falls....
There for me the Savior stands,
Shows his wounds and spreads his hands.
God is love! I know, I feel;
Jesus weeps and loves me still.
Now incline me to repent,
Let me now my sins lament,
Now my foul revolt deplore,
Weep, believe, and sin no more.

—Charles Wesley

The confession of evil works is the first beginning of good works.

—Augustine

June 13

O send out your light and your truth;
let them lead me;
let them bring me to your holy hill
and to your dwelling.

Psalm 43:3

Lead me, dear Lord. I need your light shining on the road ahead of me. Life is complicated these days, and I don't know where to turn. Illuminate the options for me. Let me see which path to take. I need your truth ringing in my ears. So many voices these days woo me this way or that way, I don't know whom to believe. Except you. I trust your Word, and I trust you to guide me through my current straits.

The Lord went in front of them in a pillar of cloud by day, to lead them along the way, and in a pillar of fire by night, to give them light, so that they might travel by day and by night.

—Exodus 13:21

June 14

May he grant you your heart's desire,
and fulfill all your plans.
May we shout for joy over your victory,
and in the name of our God set up our banners.

Psalm 20:4–5

I pray today for those stepping out into new ventures, especially those who are seeking new ways to serve you. Go with them, Lord. Guide them in the planning process, and grant them success. Encourage them when things don't work out at first, and help them keep their heads when they encounter the first flush of success. Along with the psalmist, I want to "shout for joy" and wave flags to celebrate their victory. Please, Lord, honor the desires of your servants to serve you more effectively.

He brought me to the banqueting house,
and his banner over me *was* love.

—Song of Songs 2:4 (KJV)

177

June 15

My times are in your hand;
deliver me from the hand of my enemies and persecutors.

Psalm 31:15

Why does life get increasingly difficult, my Lord? Not all the time, of course. There are times of joy and pleasure, but how quickly things turn. A bad break, an angry word, a new threat  to fret over, and suddenly each day is a struggle. It's hard to get out of bed in the morning. I know life has its ups and downs, but I could stand a few more ups and a lot fewer downs. Let me remember, Lord, that "my times are in your hand." You ride that roller coaster with me, don't you? Good times and bad, you have a handle on them all.

David knew well that the times belonged to the Lord. That's why he refused to kill King Saul when he had the chance, because it was up to the Lord to determine the limits of Saul's reign.

June 16

*R*elationships are truly beautiful. Relationships are difficult. I guess you know that, Lord, since most of the Bible describes your passionate love for humanity. Today I bring before you my closest relationships. You know both their beauty and their challenges. You understand the pleasure I draw from their love and also the anxiety. I ask you to stand behind these connections. Show us how to get along. Help us listen to each other and to you. Give us patience, wisdom, and creativity. Share with us your secrets of sacrificial love.

Love is patient; love is kind; love is not envious or boastful or arrogant or rude. It does not insist on its own way; it is not irritable or resentful; it does not rejoice in wrongdoing, but rejoices in the truth. It bears all things, believes all things, hopes all things, endures all things.

—1 Corinthians 13:4–7

June 17

With all the Father's Day ads, I think of you, the Father of all creation. Yet I realize that there are all kinds of fathers in this world. Some are absent or abusive; some are distant or demanding; and some are caring and giving. When some people think of you as a father, fear and anger consumes them. But here the psalmist calls you "father of orphans." For anyone who needs a good father, you step in. Whatever failings any earthly father has, you make up for that earthly father. There is genuine fatherly love available to us all. Thank you, my "heavenly dad."

June 18

For you, O Lord, are my hope,
my trust, O Lord, from my youth.

Psalm 71:5

O God, our help in ages past, our hope for
  years to come,
Our shelter from the stormy blast, and our eternal
  home!
Under the shadow of thy throne, still may we dwell
  secure;
Sufficient is thine arm alone, and our defense is sure.
Before the hills in order stood, or earth received
  her frame,
From everlasting, thou art God, to endless years
  the same.

—Isaac Watts

Hope is the expectation of good things to come.

June 19

I have been young, and now am old,
yet I have not seen the righteous forsaken
or their children begging bread.

Psalm 37:25

Through the years, supreme Lord, you have provided. I thank you for that. You have proven faithful again and again. I'm not just talking about material things—food, clothing, a home, and a job. You provide such blessings according to your wisdom, but, more than that, you provide strength to get us through tough times, you provide faith to focus on your spiritual blessings, and you provide joy in relationships with you and your people. Your promise is clear: A family that bases its life on your righteous love will not be forsaken. You will bless them with your spiritual blessings from generation to generation.

The best blessing that parents give their children is an honest, living faith. Don't hide flaws, market the faith, or look only at the bright side. It is the stark reality of God's presence that will win them.

June 20

Come, O children, listen to me;
I will teach you the fear of the Lord.

Psalm 34:11

What does it mean to "fear" you, Lord? To cower? To run away from your awesome power? To hide from your righteous gaze? It can't be those things, can it? You invite us to draw near to you and to love you. Yes, I am in awe of your power. Your holiness humbles me. You are God, and I know I am not. But my shrinking back is overcome by my attraction to you. This is how I "fear" you, by paying attention to you every day, living out my love for you. This is what I want to teach my family—and everyone in the next generation: "Children, don't run away from God in terror! Instead, draw near to him in humble love."

There is no fear in love, but perfect love casts out fear.

—1 John 4:18

183

June 21

As far as the east is from the west,
so far he removes our transgressions from us.

Psalm 103:12

Most Holy God, I'm amazed by your capacity for forgiveness. We both know that I have wronged you. I come before you as a sinner, depending on your mercy. Thankfully, you lift me up and treat me as a friend. My transgressions are gone, completely discarded in the other direction. You hold no grudge. You have wiped the slate clean, allowing us to move forward in our relationship. Thank you, my dear, dear Lord. And please give me that same ability to forgive, because I can't do it on my own. When others offend me, help me forgive them with an open heart.

God made you alive together with [Christ], when he forgave us all our trespasses, erasing the record that stood against us with its legal demands. He set this aside, nailing it to the cross.

—Colossians 2:13–14

June 22

*Do not be far from me,
for trouble is near
and there is no one to help.*

Psalm 22:11

*W*e beseech thee, Master, to be our helper
and protector.
Save the afflicted among us;
have mercy on the lowly;
raise up the fallen;
appear to the needy;
heal the ungodly;
restore the wanderers of thy people;
feed the hungry;
ransom our prisoners;
raise up the sick;
comfort the faint-hearted.

—Clement of Rome

Remember, I am with you always,
to the end of the age.

—Matthew 28:20

185

June 23

I wash my hands in innocence,
and go around your altar, O Lord,
singing aloud a song of thanksgiving,
and telling all your wondrous deeds.

Psalm 26:6–7

My Lord, it is a great feeling to bask in your presence. There have been times when I have come to you wracked with guilt or weighed down with worry, but you have assured me that my sin is forgiven and that you will care for me. So the burden is off my back. I am free and  clear. I feel like singing. I lift up my soul to worship you in a wholehearted expression of praise and love, and I will share your greatness with anyone who will listen. You are an awesome God!

These verses from Psalm 26 obviously refer to a range of worship activities, possibly by priests or Levites—the ritual washing, the offering of sacrifices, and singing and proclaiming. We can all understand the joy of entering worship with a pure heart and declaring our love for the Lord.

June 24

Depart from evil, and do good;
seek peace, and pursue it.

Psalm 34:14

*H*elp me, dear Lord, to seek peace. That might mean I have to back down from a fight. It might mean I don't get my way. It might mean that I don't have to be right all the time. I don't have to win. Help me put aside my selfish goals and consider the needs of others. Give me a sense of what *you* want in every situation.

Blessed are the peacemakers, for they will be called children of God.

—Matthew 5:9

June 25

Sing to him a new song;
play skillfully on the strings, with loud shouts.

Psalm 33:3

I like the old songs, almighty God. I know how to sing those. The new ones have different rhythms. They take my voice to places it isn't used to going. But I sing them anyway, because it pleases you. What is it about you, Lord, that wants newness all the time? Why does everything have to be fresh and creative with you? Just when I get used to some sort of pattern in my life, something I can count on, you shake it up with a new challenge, as well as a new blessing. Help me see your hand in the new things I don't yet understand and praise you for making all things—including my life—new and beautiful.

The steadfast love of the Lord never ceases,
his mercies never come to an end;
they are new every morning.

—Lamentations 3:22–23

June 26

For his anger is but for a moment;
his favor is for a lifetime.
Weeping may linger for the night,
but joy comes with the morning.

Psalm 30:5

When bad things happen, my Lord, I'm full of questions. Why? If "God is love," and I believe you are, how can you let us suffer like this? It doesn't make sense. I twist and turn it in my mind, and there's no way to make sense of it. If you are Lord of all, and I believe you are, can't you prevent disaster? Or are you punishing us for some reason? I don't get it. But then the dawn breaks with . . . not an answer exactly, but a kind of whisper. "Trust me and love me." You invite me into this lifetime relationship that's based not on understanding but on loving faith. I may never figure you out, Lord, but I'll keep talking with you about it. And please keep whispering to me.

Blessed are those who mourn,
for they will be comforted.

—Matthew 5:4

June 27

Humility? I've got that covered, Lord.
I'm the humblest person in town. No,
seriously, I need your help in sorting out this whole
self-esteem issue. Is it all right for me to feel good
about who I am? After all, I'm created by you *in
your image!* What's more, you have redeemed me
and filled me with your Spirit. You have even given
me certain abilities to use for your glory. I'm not
boasting about any of this, but I'm appreciating it.
Yet, Lord, I want to stay humble, to keep learning
from you. Let me never assume that I know
everything I need to know. Let me never claim
to have attained some great level of spirituality.
Whatever I am, it's your doing. I know that. I just
want to feel good about being the person you've
made me.

The problem with humility is . . . once
you think you have it, you don't.

June 28

*Some take pride in chariots, and some in horses,
but our pride is in the name of the Lord our God.*

Psalm 20:7

I see prideful people all around me, righteous Lord. The "chariots" they boast about are often sports cars. It's not horses they take pride in, but houses. They flaunt their gadgets. They preen in their high-fashion garb. These are all symbols of their power. And yes, Lord, sometimes I get caught up in that too, either boasting about what I have or coveting what I don't. But I now renounce all of that. You are the one who made me. You are the one who loves me. You are the one who gives my life meaning. If I ever forget that, forgive me and remind me of the truth. I am your child, and that is all I need to boast about.

Trust in the Lord with all your heart,
and do not rely on your own insight.
In all your ways acknowledge him,
and he will make straight your paths.

—Proverbs 3:5–6

191

June 29

He made my feet like the feet of a deer,
and set me secure on the heights.

Psalm 18:33

y Lord, how easy it is to slip and fall. One minute I'm riding high, enjoying the blessings of life, and suddenly I crash to earth. Sometimes my own pride does me in. Sometimes I forget about you, Lord.

Sometimes, like Peter walking on the sea, I pay more attention to the wind and waves than to you. Is there a way to stay up there in those "mountaintop experiences"? But it's not really the "experience" I want to hold onto, it's you. Please stay close to me, Lord, whether I'm feeling high or low. In the heights and in the depths, you are the one I cling to.

The psalmist refers to the mountain deer, whose hooves are designed to grip the rocky terrain of Israel's mountains. That's what our faith in Jesus should be like.

June 30

Be gracious to me, O Lord, for I am languishing;
O Lord, heal me, for my bones are shaking with terror.

Psalm 6:2

Terror has been all over the news in recent years, supreme Lord, and I admit it affects me too. I find myself worrying about this world, but I'm especially anxious about the well-being of my loved ones. It's not just terrorism, Lord, but health care, finances, and aging. What's ahead for us? What will the future bring? Grace. Healing. Your loving touch. Thank you, Lord, for the surety of your active presence.

We don't know what the future holds,
but we know who holds the future.

July

July 1

Let the nations be glad and sing for joy,
for you judge the peoples with equity
and guide the nations upon earth.

Psalm 67:4

Dear Lord, I'm grateful to live among those who have enjoyed a heritage of knowing your Word, of hearing your gospel, and of acknowledging you as God. Times may be changing, but I ask that you would cause my heart to remain steadfastly devoted to you. Keep my children and grandchildren in your ways, and draw to yourself the hearts of those who have become lost in following after things other than you. Strengthen your people as they follow you, and may they be beacons of your light to those who dwell in darkness.

Faithful people have always lived this way. They take care of their home and family, participate in society and government, raise children, and have occupations in agriculture, commerce, and industry. All the while, they realize that they, like their ancestors, are temporary residents of a foreign land.

—Martin Luther, *Faith Alone: A Daily Devotional*

July 2

For God is the king of all the earth;
sing praises with a psalm.
God is king over the nations;
God sits on his holy throne.

Psalm 47:7–8

Receive my wishes, O Lord, my God, and my desires of giving Thee infinite praise and immense blessings, which according to the multitude of Thine unspeakable greatness, are most justly due Thee.

These I render, and desire to render Thee every day and every moment; and I invite and entreat all the heavenly spirits, and all the faithful, with my prayers and affections, to join with me in giving Thee praises and thanks.

—Thomas à Kempis,
The Imitation of Christ

As I rejoice in God's greatness today, I am not alone. Heaven continually sings his praises; I join a heavenly host when I sing to him. The earth, too, is full of his glory and thus praises him; I join an earthly host, as well, when I seek to glorify my Lord and King.

July 3

The counsel of the Lord stands forever,
the thoughts of his heart to all generations.

Psalm 33:11

Who has known the mind of God? And yet, Lord, you have revealed to us a glimpse of what you are like through the counsel of your true and eternal Word. Help me search out and value the thoughts of your heart by studying the Scriptures. Open my heart and mind to the wonders of your self-disclosure. May I love and search it out like a buried treasure. And may my example of loving your Word inspire a new generation to seek you out as well.

"For who has known the mind of the Lord so as to instruct him?" But we have the mind of Christ.

—1 Corinthians 2:16

197

July 4

Thank you for blessing my life through your sovereign purposes for this nation in which I live. Remind me today, heavenly Father, that the values of justice, righteousness, and equity originate with you and will be ultimately and finally established by you one day. So please help me live in light of them now, walking justly and uprightly while seeking mercy for those who are in need of it. And I pray you would guide this nation, along with the other nations of earth, to

seek you out and serve you with reverence and gratitude.

O beautiful for spacious skies,
For amber waves of grain,
For purple mountain majesties
Above the fruited plain!
America! America!
God shed His grace on thee,
And crown thy good with brotherhood
From sea to shining sea!

—Katherine L. Bates, "America, the Beautiful"

July 5

Let your steadfast love, O Lord, be upon us,
even as we hope in you.

Psalm 33:22

ear Father, I long to live in a nation that looks to you and walks in ways of truth and love, ways that lead to peace and authentic unity among those who hope in you. Please renew my heart in the things that please you, so I can be the kind of citizen that makes such a nation possible.

We all have a duty to work for peace. But in order to achieve peace, we should learn from Jesus to be meek and humble of heart. Only humility will lead us to unity, and unity will lead to peace.

—Mother Teresa, *In My Own Words*

July 6

Our soul waits for the Lord;
he is our help and shield.
Our heart is glad in him,
because we trust in his holy name.

Psalm 33:20–21

ord Jesus, while
you were on the
earth, you reminded us that
there would be wars and
we would hear rumors of
wars until your return. How
we look forward to the day

when you will bring your peace to fully rule over all!
Until then, we find our peace in the refuge of your
promises and in the comforting presence of your
Holy Spirit. In you, though, we don't just take cover
until you come back again, but rather we rise up in
triumphant rejoicing because we trust in you.

People will wait patiently, excitedly in line for
the release of a long-awaited product when it
hits the stores or a movie when it arrives at the
box office. How much more should we have
that attitude today as we await the Lord's
promised intervention in our lives!

July 7

My flesh and my heart may fail,
but God is the strength of my heart and my portion forever.

Psalm 73:26

Heavenly Father, in my weak moments when I fail to be what I should be, when I don't do what I ought to do, when I say what I shouldn't, and when I'm silent when I should speak, please intervene! Be my strength! Redeem my mistakes! Show yourself strong when I falter, and bring glory to yourself. I look to you and want to point others to you today. Use my imperfections to

highlight my great need for you, and teach me to walk in your strength and not in my own withering strength.

God generally doesn't seek out the innately strong as "poster children" for faith; it is most often the weak through whom he can best demonstrate his strength and in whom he can cultivate great faith.

July 8

For me it is good to be near God;
I have made the Lord God my refuge,
to tell of all your works.

Psalm 73:28

Father in Heaven! Draw our hearts to Thee, that our heart may be where our treasure must be that our thoughts may aspire to Thy kingdom where our citizenship is so that our departure when Thou shalt call us may not be a painful separation from  this world but a blissful reunion with Thee.... O Lord our God, teach us and strengthen this conviction in our hearts, that also in this life, we belong to Thee. Amen.

—Søren Kierkegaard,
"We Belong to Thee"

Knowing God intimately is to have many stories to tell of his goodness.

July 9

*Glorious are you, more majestic
than the everlasting mountains.*

Psalm 76:4

We salute the kings of the earth with
"Your Majesty." How much more worthy
are you of that honor than they, Lord! How regal
are your works, such as the mountains! How they
reflect your own majestic nature! And yet in another
sense, only dimly, for I'm aware that a full revelation
of your glory would be my undoing. Thank you that
you show me, though, what you are like in ways that
I can perceive and to which I can respond. These
revelations inspire worship and awe in my spirit
and point ahead to the day when you will make me
able to "handle" the unveiling of your majesty as I
worship in your very presence.

The truly majestic is found in few things on
earth, and yet when we encounter your majesty,
we know it immediately, instinctively. It, perhaps
more than any other quality, inspires our
worship. We must be careful, then, not to
allow ourselves to worship at the altar of
any majesty other than God's own.

203

July 10

You are the God who works wonders;
you have displayed your might among the peoples.

Psalm 77:14

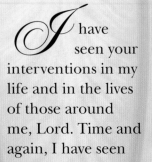

I have seen your interventions in my life and in the lives of those around me, Lord. Time and again, I have seen you heal and provide and protect and save. Help me speak up about the mighty things I've seen you do. Grant me an opportunity today to tell someone about how wonderful you are, how powerful are your works, and how good you are to me.

Miracles happen every day. It's my perspective that often misses them. Do I see the miracle of sunrise? Of a functioning body? Of a flower blooming or the changing seasons? May the Lord change my perspective so I won't miss the miracles of his provision, protection, and salvation in my life.

July 11

Help us, O God of our salvation,
for the glory of your name;
deliver us, and forgive our sins,
for your name's sake.

Psalm 79:9

*L*ord Jesus, you taught us to pray to our heavenly Father as a community, using "our" and "us" in the prayer you taught your disciples. Help me remember to pray in an attitude that is concerned for the welfare of the entire community of faith. We belong to you, and in you we are united as one body. Together and individually, we are identified with you, called by your name, and in need of your daily help and intervention in our lives. And O, how we need you! Be pleased to glorify yourself today through the ways you bring salvation to us.

Jesus Christ brings freedom to your total person, and even your individuality is transformed. The transformation is brought about by love—personal devotion to Jesus. Love is the overflowing result of one person in true fellowship with another.

—Oswald Chambers

205

July 12

Restore us, O Lord God of hosts;
let your face shine, that we may be saved.

Psalm 80:19

My Lord, it seems as if the ways of honor and respect, faith and love that we once practiced as a culture have been steadily declining. I pray that even if they are one day completely abandoned, all those who put their trust in you will faithfully walk in your ways and be as lights and sources of goodness to minister your blessing to our neighbors. Forgive us for ways we have compromised and abandoned what we know is right. Save us from our apathy and our affections for things that are opposed to you. Please restore our conscience and our desire to follow you wholeheartedly. In your holy name, I pray. Amen.

Restoration may be a process, but the *way* of restoration is just one step away—a single decision to leave our own path and get in step with God's Spirit.

July 13

*O Lord my God, I cried to you for help,
and you have healed me.*

Psalm 30:2

hank you for all the ways in which you bring healing into my life, dear Lord. My heart, soul, mind, and body find new strength in you each day. Sometimes the healing you bring is sudden, sometimes incremental, and sometimes it is the promise of my ultimate healing for which I must wait. But I thank you for all these ways of yours. I'm grateful for how they tether me to you, keep me near you, and cultivate the relationship with you that I so desperately need. Each time I cry to you for help, I am more convinced than ever that you hear me and answer me according to what I need most.

If we insist on what we want in the way of healing—without allowing for God's will to be done in the process—we may, in our limited perspective, miss the miracle of how he does things, which are not as we expected but as he planned them in his perfect wisdom for our good and his glory.

July 14

Give justice to the weak and the orphan;
maintain the right of the lowly and the destitute.

Psalm 82:3

Great and good Father, increase my concern for those who need practical intervention in their lives and who may need the help of another person to encourage or teach or defend or shelter them in some way. Bring these vulnerable ones to

my attention, and though I may not be able to provide everything they need, show me what you would have me offer that would demonstrate your care. Grant me your own compassion and willingness to give of myself for the sake of another. In Jesus' name, I pray. Amen.

As I help others, I cultivate a spirit of helpfulness and love in those around me—in my children, in neighbors, in coworkers, and in my community.

July 15

For a day in your courts is better
than a thousand elsewhere.
I would rather be a doorkeeper in the house of my God
than live in the tents of wickedness.

Psalm 84:10

lmighty Father, the ways of the world offer a dose of short-lived fun, followed by a sentence of long-term sorrow. Please keep me from "buying in" to the world's lies. Help me focus my intentions and desires on the path of life to which you call me. It may not seem glamorous at a temporal glance, but the wonders and joys you offer are deep and pure and profound, lasting for all eternity and satisfying the true desires of my heart. Thank you for the peace and promise of living in your presence.

The ways of the world are those that look like candy but turn out to be the bitterest of pills. The ways of Christ, on the contrary, may seem a bitter pill in the beginning, but they lead us to an exquisite feast.

July 16

For the Lord God is a sun and shield;
he bestows favor and honor.
No good thing does the Lord withhold
from those who walk uprightly.

Psalm 84:11

*L*ord God, help me walk uprightly today—not to impress anyone else or to make myself feel morally superior to those around me. Help me walk uprightly that I might enjoy fellowship with you as you intend it so that nothing may hinder our joy of communing together throughout the day. If others see your light shining in me, may they be drawn to you. If your blessing comes through an act of love or obedience, give me a thankful heart that you have upheld me in your righteousness. Grant me true humility as you teach me to walk in your ways. It is because you are good that I can walk with you. Thank you for all of your blessings!

Attribute to God all that is good, and walk in his goodness as in the light of a beacon to which you can quickly point if someone notices how bright your way is.

July 17

Let me hear what God the Lord will speak,
for he will speak peace to his people,
to his faithful, to those who turn to him in their hearts.

Psalm 85:8

My Lord, teach me to listen. The times are noisy and my ears are weary with the thousand raucous sounds which continuously assault them.... Let me hear Thee speaking in my heart. Let me get used to the sounds of Thy voice, that its tones may be familiar when the sounds of earth die away and the only sound will be the music of Thy speaking voice. Amen.

—A. W. Tozer,
The Pursuit of God

If I should stop to listen to God for one minute in each waking hour of the day, I would be devoting 16 minutes a day to hearing the voice of God. Is there a quarter-hour block of time in my day I could devote to listening to God, even if on some days he chooses to sit with me in silence?

July 18

Almighty God...bless our land with honourable industry, sound learning, and pure manners. Save us from violence, discord, and confusion; from pride and arrogancy, and from every evil way. Defend our liberties, and fashion into one united people the multitudes brought hither out of many kindreds and tongues. Endure with the spirit of wisdom those to whom in Thy Name we entrust the authority of government, that there may be justice and peace at home, and that, through obedience to Thy law, we may show forth Thy praise among the nations of the earth. In the time of prosperity, fill our hearts with thankfulness, and in the day of trouble, suffer not our trust in Thee to fail. Amen.

—George L. Locke

We cannot earn God's favor, but God is pleased to bless those who seek to honor him.

July 19

Teach me your way, O Lord,
that I may walk in your truth;
give me an undivided heart to revere your name.

Psalm 86:11

My Lord, the things that tempt my heart away from undivided devotion to you are the things of this world that offer temporary comfort, pleasure, or a boost to my ego. It's when I turn to these things for what I need instead of to you that I put them in a place they do not belong. Please make me aware of the ways in which I am fashioning idols out of other things, whether out of your kind provisions or things expressly forbidden. Turn my heart fully toward you so that my way may not be darkened by the deceptiveness of false ways.

If a house divided against itself cannot stand, neither can a divided heart keep to a single purpose.

July 20

I will walk with integrity of heart
within my house;
I will not set before my eyes
anything that is base.

Psalm 101:2–3

I Pray Heaven to Bestow The Best of Blessing on THIS HOUSE, and on ALL that shall hereafter Inhabit it. May none but Honest and Wise Men ever rule under This Roof!

—President John Adams's letter to his wife, Abigail, the day after he moved into the White House (November 2, 1800)

May we, as individuals, adopt this prayer for our own homes. For there is no house of government that can ever be as influential as our family homes are, nor can what transpires in government mansions be as important as what is modeled, taught, and "caught" within the sacred walls of our own households.

July 21

But I, O Lord, cry out to you;
in the morning my prayer comes before you.

Psalm 88:13

When I wake up with my needs standing before me, Lord, standing right where I left them when I fell asleep, let prayer be my first response. As I lift my soul to you right now, let me continue to lift it all day long. From the time my alarm clock sounds to get up to the time I set it again at bedtime, may my prayers rise up to you as though in a continual conversation with a beloved

friend, for that is what you have called me—your beloved and your friend. My love returns to you today as I seek you and consult you in all things.

Our spiritual need to pray is comparable to our physical need to breathe.

July 22

Turn, O Lord! How long?
Have compassion on your servants!
Psalm 90:13

*I*t is oftentimes a small thing which casts me down and troubles me.... Strengthen me with heavenly fortitude, lest the old man, the miserable flesh, not fully subject to the spirit, prevail and get the upper hand, against which we must fight as long as we breathe in this most wretched life.

—Thomas à Kempis, *The Imitation of Christ*

When life seems unbearable, sometimes the best thing we can do is stop trying to bear it ourselves and cast ourselves, headlong with our circumstances, on God. This is not "escapism" or denial; it is simply faith in action.

July 23

Who rises up for me against the wicked?
Who stands up for me against evildoers?

Psalm 94:16

Dear Lord, grant me courage to stand up for what is right, true, and good, even if no one else will join me. Help me not waver or become afraid of opposition. Uphold and establish me in your Word and your ways. I am not strong, but in your strength I can do all things. For your honor and glory, not my own, I pray. Amen.

To do what is right is to side with the truth of God. And never doubt it, the truth of God will always prevail. Evil may cause setbacks, and it may hamper the steady march of God's plan, but it is ultimately powerless to stop it. To do what is right is to join the winning side of the fight though the battle will not be without pain or struggle.

—Chuck Swindoll, *A Life Well Lived*

July 24

The Lord loves those who hate evil;
he guards the lives of his faithful;
he rescues them from the hand of the wicked.

Psalm 97:10

The presence of evil in the world, Lord, is often used as an argument against your existence, but your Word tells me that while evil  plagues humanity as a result of our wrong choices, you remain thoroughly good. I know you promise to establish good once and for all at the end of time, but for now, as evil and good coexist on earth, help me embrace that which is good, while turning away from what is evil. Today, as you call me to walk in your righteousness, may I respond with a willing heart. By your grace, I pray. Amen.

Those who belong to God share his delight in what is good, his disdain for what is wicked, and his love for all people.

July 25

Mighty King, lover of justice,
you have established equity;
you have executed justice
and righteousness.

Psalm 99:4

Sovereign Lord, vindicate me when I have borne injustices, but even more importantly, remind me to speak and act in ways that are just and equitable toward others. Help me give people the same respect and right dealings I desire in my interactions with them. In that way, I can reflect your own character that loves what is just, right, and fair.

The deeds we do, the words we say,
Into still air they seem to fleet,
We count them ever past;
But they shall last,
In the dread judgment they
And we shall meet.

—John Keble, *The Effect of Example*

July 26

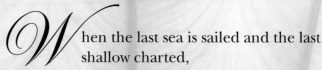

Light dawns for the righteous,
and joy for the upright in heart.

Psalm 97:11

When the last sea is sailed and the last
        shallow charted,
    When the last field is reaped and the last
harvest stored,
    When the last fire is out and the last guest
departed,
    Grant the last prayer that I shall pray,
Be good to me, O Lord.

—Masefield, *D'Avalos' Prayer*

The day that dawns in heaven for me will never know a
sunset. In its eternal light, I will always live and rejoice
without fear or pain or dread or sorrow or worry, with no
shadow of death lurking and looming anymore. I shall
soar in unmitigated joy and then light in pure peace and
sing clearly and dance freely as I was created to do. I will
be united at last with the love of my life and never again
be separated from him nor from any of those who
have loved him on earth. And so shall we ever
be with the Lord, for the day that dawns in
heaven for us will never know a sunset.

July 27

*So teach us to count our days
that we may gain a wise heart.*

Psalm 90:12

My Lord, my days on earth have a number. That number is unknown to me or to anyone else but you. What I do know, however, is that I have this moment in which I can seek you, seek to know you, and seek to walk in your wisdom. Please help me not squander or fritter away the time that you have granted me to live. I want to go about my days purposefully, yet with a light and joyful spirit, as I entrust myself to you and obey your Word and your Spirit in all things.

Twelve-step recovery programs urge participants to take life one day, one moment, at a time. There is great wisdom in this, since none of us can retrieve the past nor can we know the future; we can only live and act in this present moment—the gift of life granted to us right now.

July 28

Know that the Lord is God.
It is he that made us, and we are his;
we are his people, and the sheep of his pasture.

Psalm 100:3

My precious Lord, what does it mean to *know* that you are God? The psalm for today gives me some clues: to remember that I'm not my own, that I belong to you, and that you made me. That's a start. I'll begin there, Lord, and thank you for making me. I'm thankful that I am one of your "sheep" and that you are such a kind and good shepherd, who with wisdom and patience tends to all that pertains to my life. You are God, indeed. Help me pause often to remember it so that I won't get off track and wander from your kind and perfect purposes for my life.

I am the good shepherd. I know my own and my own know me, just as the Father knows me and I know the Father. And I lay down my life for the sheep.

John 10:14–15

July 29

For he is our God,
and we are the people of his pasture,
and the sheep of his hand.

Psalm 95:7

  Father in Heaven!…Grant us to feel that without Thee we can do nothing—a feeling not of cowardly dependence but a feeling of hopeful strength, in the happy assurance that Thou art powerful among the weak.

—Søren Kierkegaard, "Our Dependence on Thee"

Sheep are completely dependent on their shepherd's protection, provision, guidance, doctoring, knowledge of the land, and kindness. They trust only their shepherd and will answer the call of no other.

July 30

As a father has compassion for his children,
so the Lord has compassion for those who fear him.
For he knows how we are made;
he remembers that we are dust.

Psalm 103:13–14

Sometimes I want to believe that I'm made of physical and moral titanium, Lord, but I'm not. My best efforts are more like wood, hay, and stubble. It's only because of your mercy and grace at work in my life that I see good spiritual fruit being produced there. Thank you that you remember (and you remind me) I'm made of mere earthly elements, and my body will someday return to the dust. Thank you that, knowing my frailties, you are compassionate toward me. I receive your kindness with deep gratitude today.

Humility acknowledges God and opens the door for his compassion to flow into my life.

July 31

The steadfast love of the Lord is from everlasting to everlasting
on those who fear him,
and his righteousness to children's children.

Psalm 103:17

Almighty Father, in a world where everything seems to be changing by the minute, the word "steadfast" is like a neon sign, indicating a  place of refuge. And that is what your love is, Lord: a refuge, the one thing we can count on in life and the thing that doesn't change. I never know what the price of fuel will be in the morning, but I know I will wake up with the assurance of your love. May each successive generation—my children, grandchildren, great-grandchildren, and beyond—come to know the assurance of your steadfast love.

It is said that, in life, only death and taxes are certain, but what is truly certain in this life? For starters, God's love and his faithfulness. How much better are these certainties than the other supposed ones! How much better life seems in light of them!

August

August 1

Your decrees are wonderful;
therefore my soul keeps them.

Psalm 119:129

I know I resist you sometimes, Lord, but I have to admit that I need your guidance. When I follow your lead, my life is far better. When I follow the teachings of your Word, I have a sense of purpose, a sense of order, and a sense of connection. You have challenged me to love others, and we both know this isn't always easy for me to do—especially with *some* of the "others." But when I reach out with a kind word or do a helpful deed, the results are wonderful to behold, and things fall into place. So help me obey you more often.

If we walk in the light as he himself is in the light, we have fellowship with one another, and the blood of Jesus his Son cleanses us from all sin.

—1 John 1:7

August 2

I was glad when they said to me,
"Let us go to the house of the Lord!"

Psalm 122:1

Thank you, Lord, for
the place I can go
Reserved for the worship of you.
Thank you for people who
gather to know
What's honest, eternal, and
true.
Thank you for love that exudes
from that site,
Blessing my life in all ways.
I join in the worship, I feel the delight,
I offer a heart full of praise.

Sometimes skeptics say, "The church is full of
hypocrites." Well, sure, but can you think of
a better place for hypocrites to be? We sin in
many ways, including hypocrisy, but we keep
coming back to receive grace from our God.

August 3

The ordinances of the Lord are true
and righteous altogether.
More to be desired are they than gold,
even much fine gold;
sweeter also than honey,
and drippings of the honeycomb.

Psalm 19:9–10

Great God, you spoke the universe into being. "Let there be light!" you declared, and suddenly there was light. Ever since, you've been speaking the light into our lives. I thank you for being a God who communicates. You do not sit far off in some celestial retreat waiting for us to try to figure you out. No, you have spoken to us through the prophets and apostles, and your Spirit brings the Scriptures to life in our hearts. Your words are sweet to me. They fill me with joy and satisfaction. Keep speaking to me, dear Lord. I am listening.

For it is the God who said, "Let light shine out of darkness," who has shone in our hearts to give the light of the knowledge of the glory of God in the face of Jesus Christ.

—2 Corinthians 4:6

229

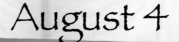

August 4

The Lord is my shepherd, I shall not want.

Psalm 23:1

The King of Love my shepherd is, whose
goodness faileth never.
I nothing lack if I am his, and he is mine forever.
Where streams of living water flow, my ransomed
soul he leadeth,
And where the verdant pastures grow, with food
celestial feedeth.
Perverse and foolish, oft I strayed, but yet in love
he sought me
And on his shoulder gently laid, and home,
rejoicing, brought me.

—Henry W. Baker

Now may the God of peace, who brought
back from the dead our Lord Jesus, the great
shepherd of the sheep, by the blood of the
eternal covenant, make you complete in
everything good so that you may do his will.

—Hebrews 13:20–21

August 5

Prove me, O Lord, and try me;
test my heart and mind.
For your steadfast love is before my eyes,
and I walk in faithfulness to you.

Psalm 26:2–3

Merciful Lord, I understand the concept of testing. I tie a knot and yank on it to make sure it will hold. I have vivid memories of difficult exams in school that seemed to turn my brain inside out and shake it to see what would come out. I don't have a lot of experience with smelting, but I know that metal goes into the furnace and it comes out stronger. I get it. Being tested is good for us. But it's still tough to go through. I don't know what kind of test you're putting me through right now, but I hope it's over soon. And I hope I'll pass the test and that I'll come out of it stronger, wiser, and closer to you. But I have to tell you, I'm not sure I'm going to make it. Please, God, help me!

[God] knows the way that I take; when he has
tested me, I will come forth as gold.

—Job 23:10 (NIV)

August 6

I trust in you, O Lord;
I say, "You are my God."

Psalm 31:14

look around at my neighbors, dear Lord, and I wonder where they're putting their trust. They work hard and earn money, trying to buy some measure of happiness. They seek security in insurance policies and alarm systems. They seem to worship cars, computers, and weekends. I'm not saying I'm any better than they are. You know how often I get swayed that way, but, Lord, I declare right now that you are my God. I want no other gods before you. You are the one I trust in—you alone.

The first of the Ten Commandments is the anchor for all the others. When God is God, and we worship no other, the rest of our life falls into place.

232

August 7

Let all the earth fear the Lord;
let all the inhabitants of the world stand in awe of him.
For he spoke, and it came to be;
he commanded, and it stood firm.

Psalm 33:8–9

You are an awesome God! I confess I should spend more time in awe of you. Forgive me, Lord, if I get too chummy, treating you like a casual pal, someone I can take for granted. Yes, you describe yourself as a loving father with the yearnings of a compassionate mother. You say you're a friend of sinners like me, and I take you at your word. So I'm not apologizing for enjoying your love. I'm just acknowledging that you are also the awesome Creator of the universe. Let me never forget your amazing power. Let me never stop hailing your extraordinary majesty. You, my God, are the King above all kings—and still, amazingly, you love me. Thank you.

We need a new word in English, something between *fear* and *friendship*—a word that captures our overwhelming awe in the presence of a great God but also accepts his invitation to intimacy. Perhaps that word is *worship*.

August 8

Sovereign Lord, I need your help. I have come to the end of my own ability. You know the situation I'm in, the problems I'm having, and the obstacles I face. I need a miracle! Please step in to help. I've tried to fix things myself, but I've made things worse. Whenever I forge ahead in my

own direction, I do damage. So I'm appealing to you. I need you now. I've always needed you, but now I realize how much. Don't be a stranger to me. I invite you to step in and work your wonders in my situation. And for whatever I do, I will give you all the glory.

August 9

*O Lord, all my longing is known to you;
my sighing is not hidden from you.*

Psalm 38:9

Ah, Lord, my life appears to be entirely good, but it's really not. I could count my blessings and fill up a notepad or two, but you know the problems I have, too. Sometimes I sigh with deep dissatisfaction. *If only... Why did I...? Why couldn't things have turned out differently?* My heart has plenty of regrets and remorse, and I do my share of coveting and gazing at the green grass on the other side of the fence. Ah, Lord, I take comfort in the fact that you know all that's in my heart—good and bad. Whisper your peace to me. Fill all my longings with your delightful presence.

Every morning, God's mercy is brand new. He hits the reset button, erasing yesterday's regrets and charting a new course. Don't get bogged down in old longings. What is God putting in your heart *today?*

235

August 10

He does not deal with us according to our sins,
nor repay us according to our iniquities.

Psalm 103:10

Heavenly Father, I'm still not sure I really understand forgiveness. I know all about right and wrong, and I try to do what's right. I see that misbehavior on my part brings bad results. I'm deeply sorry for the sins I've committed, and I know I deserve your punishment. But instead of punishing me, you forgive. You take the penalty upon yourself, and you invite me to live in a loving relationship with you. You have every right to banish me from your presence, but instead you welcome me in. It is truly amazing! Humbly, I thank you.

Just as I am, thy love unknown
hath broken every barrier down;
now, to be thine, yea, thine alone,
O Lamb of God, I come, I come.

—Charlotte Elliot

August 11

Not to us, O Lord, not to us, but to your name give glory,
for the sake of your steadfast love and your faithfulness.

Psalm 115:1

All that I have, all that I am, I lay it down
at your feet, dear Lord. All my victories,
all my accomplishments, I owe them all to you. You
have made me, you have redeemed me, and you give
me strength to live each day. Without you behind
me, supporting me, and within me, empowering me,
I would have nothing to offer. So it makes perfect
sense to offer it all back to you. Receive the glory
for whatever good things have been done through
me. Receive eternal praise for the way you have
molded this lump of clay. And please receive my
undying thanks.

Whatever gains I had, these I have come to
regard as loss because of Christ. More than
that, I regard everything as loss because
of the surpassing value of knowing
Christ Jesus my Lord.

—Philippians 3:7–8

August 12

How weighty to me are your thoughts, O God!
How vast is the sum of them!
I try to count them—they are more than the sand;
I come to the end—I am still with you.

Psalm 139:17–18

*J*ust when I think I have you figured out, almighty God, you surprise me. I keep trying to define you, to identify your systems of behavior, and to box you in—but you break out of all those boxes. I have to throw my hands up and admit that you are beyond my comprehension. And I wouldn't have it any other way. Indeed, you are overwhelmingly merciful. You have awesome power and sweet tenderness. You thunder and whisper. Your truth includes both the complex equation of the scientist and the simple song of a child. I kneel in wonder before you.

For as the heavens are higher than the earth,
so are my ways higher than your ways
and my thoughts than your thoughts.

—Isaiah 55:9

August 13

As a deer longs for flowing streams,
so my soul longs for you, O God.
My soul thirsts for God,
for the living God.

Psalm 42:1–2

My Lord, I can relate my own spiritual life to the imagery of this psalm. Not all the time, of course. Sometimes the living water flows freely and my cup overflows with your sweet presence. But my soul moves through arid patches too—spiritual deserts where your blessings seem far, far away. I'm not sure why it happens like this.

Whatever the cause, those are tough times, and I hope I don't have too many of them. I rely on your promise that I'll find you if I seek with all my heart. I yearn for your refreshing presence.

"Let anyone who is thirsty come to me, and let the one who believes in me drink. As the scripture has said, 'Out of the believer's heart shall flow rivers of living water.' "

—John 7:37–38

August 14

This is God,
our God forever and ever.
He will be our guide forever.

Psalm 48:14

*I*n a world with global positioning systems (GPS), we get a whole new understanding of the way you guide us, sovereign Lord. GPS lets us know exactly where we are in the world and how to get where we're going. Every day people rely on guidance from satellites to plot their course. Sometimes they ignore the advice they receive, or they're distracted, or they think they know a better way. In each case, the guidance is "recalculated," and a whole new set of instructions appears. This is what you do for us, Lord. You show us the way, with occasional recalculation. I rely on you to get where I need to go.

He leadeth me, O blessed thought!
O words with heavenly comfort fraught!
Whate'er I do, where'er I be,
still 'tis God's hand that leadeth me.

—Joseph H. Gilmore

August 15

I will sing of your might;
I will sing aloud of your steadfast love in the morning.
For you have been a fortress for me
and a refuge in the day of my distress.

Psalm 59:16

Alone with none but thee, my God,
I journey on my way.
What need I fear, when thou art near,
O king of night and day?
More safe am I within thy hand
Than if a host did round me stand.

In a time before electric lighting, nighttime was scary. Torchlight and campfire would help illuminate a traveler's way, but generally darkness reigned. If you woke up in the morning without being robbed by savage thieves or attacked by wild animals, you'd be grateful for God's protection.

August 16

O God, you are my God, I seek you,
my soul thirsts for you;
my flesh faints for you,
as in a dry and weary land where there is no water.

Psalm 63:1

My Lord, where are you? You seem far away lately. Am I doing something wrong? Should I be praying differently or more often? Have I mistreated some friend or relative? Is that why you're so distant? Do I  have a bad attitude about something? I don't know. Please let me know what the problem is so I can fix it. I long to feel your presence close to me again. Life is hard enough on its own, but I can't imagine living without you. I need to know that you're right beside me. Are you here, Lord? Please reveal yourself to me.

Be still, my soul: your best, your heavenly friend
Through thorny ways leads to a joyful end.

—Katharina von Schlegel

August 17

I will call to mind the deeds of the Lord;
I will remember your wonders of old.
I will meditate on all your work,
and muse on your mighty deeds.

Psalm 77:11–12

As I think back through my life, I see many times when you, my supreme ruler, stepped in to make things happen. Sometimes it was obvious that you were acting with miraculous power, but not always. Some of your deeds were more subtle than that. Only in hindsight do I see that you were involved. Maybe at the time I thought I was just lucky, or that I had achieved something through my own brilliance. But now I see that you were there all the time, behind the scenes, orchestrating events, bringing the right people into my life at the right time, and empowering me to do what needed to be done. Thank you for your intervention. Thank you for all the great things you have done in my life.

God moves in a mysterious way,
his wonders to perform.

—William Cowper

243

August 18

How great are your works, O Lord!
Your thoughts are very deep!

Psalm 92:5

Almighty Father, I want to learn from you. Can you teach me wisdom? I'm not talking about facts and formulas. I want to know how to see the world around me. I want to figure out what's really going on. Too often I'll be talking to someone in need and never know it. Will you teach me how to see that need? Will you make me more sensitive to people's inner longings? Will you help me sense those moments when a friend needs an encouraging word? Give me your perfect wisdom, dear Lord.

If any of you is lacking in wisdom, ask God, who gives to all generously and ungrudgingly, and it will be given you.

—James 1:5

August 19

You are my dwelling place, O Lord.
You are my home, my hearth,
Where I lay my head at night
And ease my heart.
I can unwind in your presence,
Set my burdens down,
With you, Lord, I'm free to be
Myself.
You are my place of nurture.
You are my place of nourishment.
You let me digest
My stress.
How good it is each day, dear Lord,
To come home to you.

Jesus answered him, "Those who love me
will keep my word, and my Father will
love them, and we will come to them
and make our home with them."

—John 14:23

245

August 20

Let the righteous be joyful;
let them exult before God;
let them be jubilant with joy.

Psalm 68:3

Great God on high,
I join the angels in
singing your praise. With all
creation I celebrate your artistry.
And along with all humans who
have tasted of your mercy, I
sing a song of redemption. You
are more than worthy of my
everlasting attention, dear Lord.
You bring great joy to my heart,

and now that joy is exploding back in your direction.
Hallelujah, my wonderful sovereign! Hail to you,
majestic ruler! Thank you, my beloved friend.

> Then I heard what seemed to be the voice of a
> great multitude, like the sound of many waters
> and like the sound of mighty thunderpeals,
> crying out, "Hallelujah! For the Lord our
> God the Almighty reigns. Let us rejoice
> and exult and give him the glory."
>
> —Revelation 19:6–7

August 21

You who live in the shelter of the Most High,
who abide in the shadow of the Almighty,
will say to the Lord, "My refuge and my fortress;
my God, in whom I trust."

Psalm 91:1–2

May God the Father bless us; may Christ take care of us; the Holy Ghost enlighten us all the days of our lives. The Lord be our defender and keeper of body and soul, both now and forever, to the ages of ages.

Shelter and shade were crucial considerations in ancient Palestine. The sun beat down intensely, and at times a wind blew in from Arabia like a blast furnace. Maybe today we need protection from reckless drivers and Internet scams, but the Lord protects as he always has.

August 22

Let my prayer be counted as incense before you,
and the lifting up of my hands as an evening sacrifice.

Psalm 141:2

$\mathcal{I}$n ancient times the sweet smell of incense would rise from the Israelites' houses of worship. Today I ask you to accept the sweet savor of my praises. I love you with all that I am. I devote myself to you. I honor and glorify you. I lift my heart to you, as well as my hands. Receive my praises and enjoy their aroma. They come from a sincere heart.

Thanks be to God, who in Christ always leads us in triumphal procession, and through us spreads in every place the fragrance that comes from knowing him.

—2 Corinthians 2:14

August 23

My days are like an evening shadow;
I wither away like grass.
But you, O Lord, are enthroned forever;
your name endures to all generations.

Psalm 102:11–12

Creator of the universe, you make amazing sunsets. I love to watch the colors change as the light of day fades. It's truly beautiful, but it vanishes all too quickly. I want to freeze those moments in time and enjoy them longer. Frankly, there are a lot of moments I want to savor, and they all seem to pass too quickly. Life rushes on, and age keeps gaining on me. But time is nothing to you, eternal God. And the life you offer me is everlasting. I don't need to fear the tenacious tide of time. I just need to keep investing in my future life with you.

Do not ignore this one fact, beloved, that with the Lord one day is like a thousand years, and a thousand years are like one day. The Lord is not slow about his promise, as some think of slowness, but is patient with you.

—2 Peter 3:8–9

August 24

O come, let us sing to the Lord;
let us make a joyful noise to the rock of our salvation!
Let us come into his presence with thanksgiving;
let us make a joyful noise to him with songs of praise!

Psalm 95:1–2

There are many ways I could come into your presence, Lord. I could approach you humbly, knowing that you're a holy God and I'm a sinner. I could come to you with questions. There's so much I want to learn from you. I could also enter

your presence with a wish list of prayer requests, because you really care about the desires of our hearts. But today I'm following the psalmist's example, stepping before you with a heart full of thanksgiving. You have abundantly blessed me, dear Lord, and I erupt with songs of joy and praise.

There's no better attitude
Than gratitude—
Nothing outranks
Thanks.

August 25

For the Lord is a great God,
and a great King above all gods.

Psalm 95:3

Our God, God of all humanity,
     God of heaven and earth, seas and rivers,
God of sun and moon, of all the stars,
God of high mountain and lowly valley,
God over heaven, and in heaven, and under heaven.
You have a dwelling in heaven and earth and sea
     and in all things that are in them.
You inspire all things, bring all things to life.
You are over all things, you support all things.
You make the light of the sun to shine,
You surround the moon and the stars,
You have made wells in the arid earth,
     placed dry islands in the sea.
Your Son is co-eternal with you,
And the Holy Spirit breathes in you.

—based on a prayer by St. Patrick

Indeed he is not far from each one of us. For "In
him we live and move and have our being."

—Acts 17:27–28

251

August 26

As for me, I shall behold your face in righteousness;
when I awake I shall be satisfied, beholding your likeness.

Psalm 17:15

*D*ear Lord, in my mind's eye I see the faces of people I have loved. I think of the joy it has always brought me, just to see a smile, a tilt of the head, and a glimmer in the eye. Thank you, Lord, for these loved ones, and I pray now for their well-being. But I also wonder today about what it's like to see *your* face. I know the psalmist speaks in a metaphor, but it's still fun and exciting to think about. What sort of glimmer is there in your eye?

Beloved, we are God's children now; what we will be has not yet been revealed. What we do know is this: when he is revealed, we will be like him, for we will see him as he is.

—1 John 3:2

August 27

I stretch out my hands to you;
my soul thirsts for you like a parched land.

Psalm 143:6

I call to you from deepest need.
    O Lord, hear my request.
I know I've sinned in word and deed,
But now I'm in distress.
Please overlook my errant ways,
And gaze at me with tender grace,
And help me fix this mess.
In you, dear Lord, I place my trust,
I've soured on self-reliance.
Your Spirit arms each one of us
To slay our taunting giants.
Your promises prove strong and true,
And I'd be nothing without you.
I pledge my full compliance.

—inspired by a hymn by Martin Luther,
    "Out of the Depths"

Times of need, calamity, and doubt are difficult
to go through, it's true. But time and time
again they drive us toward the Lord.

253

August 28

Posterity will serve him;
future generations will be told about the Lord,
and proclaim his deliverance to a people yet unborn,
saying that he has done it.

Psalm 22:30–31

Heavenly Father, let my life count for you, not only today and tomorrow, but also in the years to come. Can I leave a legacy that will inspire people long after I've gone? I'm not looking for personal fame here, but I want to serve you fully. So let me cast my vision forward. How will my devotion to you affect the next generation as well as the next? Use me, dear Lord, to bring the dynamic reality of you to the children in my life, not only teaching them but also empowering them to serve you in the future. It is my humble prayer that "people yet unborn" might be brought closer to you.

Keep these words that I am commanding you today in your heart. Recite them to your children and talk about them when you are at home and when you are away, when you lie down and when you rise.

—Deuteronomy 6:6–7

August 29

Though an army encamp against me,
my heart shall not fear;
though war rise up against me,
yet I will be confident.

Psalm 27:3

Sometimes it seems
that I'm fighting
a losing battle. Life gets
difficult, Lord, and it feels as
if everyone and everything
is against me. I seem to say
the wrong thing. People
misunderstand me. My daily
work is harder than it should
be. Even stoplights turn

red as I approach. What's going on? Is the entire
universe my enemy? Well, no, you are still on my
side, and you are much bigger and more powerful
than the whole rest of the universe—besides, you
made it! When the rest of my life becomes a struggle,
I can still rely on your support. Thank you, Lord.

And this is the victory that conquers
the world, our faith.

—1 John 5:4

August 30

Blessed be the Lord,
for he has wondrously shown his steadfast love to me
when I was beset as a city under siege.

Psalm 31:21

*S*upreme Creator, I know that feeling, being "under siege." It's as if everything suddenly goes against me. People who were the best of friends suddenly turn snippy. Activities I once enjoyed become arduous. But, Lord, you have continued to love me, and I thank you for your reassurance in those difficult periods. Now I ask you to help me keep an eye out for others who are feeling that way. Give me a sensitive heart to recognize the needs of those around me. Give me the courage to reach out and help.

He is the source of every mercy and the God who comforts us. He comforts us in all our troubles so that we can comfort others. When others are troubled, we will be able to give them the same comfort God has given us.

—2 Corinthians 1:3–4 (NLT)

256

August 31

Come, bless the Lord, all you servants of the Lord,
who stand by night in the house of the Lord!
Lift up your hands to the holy place,
and bless the Lord.

Psalm 134:1–2

I have received rich blessings from you,
dear Lord. I cannot count the ways you
have blessed me. But now I'm invited to bless *you*. I
love the idea that I can bring you joy by praising you,
by thanking you, and by serving you. Let me pay
you compliments for your creativity, wisdom, and
patience. I love you, Lord, and I'm deeply grateful
that you are my Lord.

Blessing involves saying and doing. God blesses us by
speaking his Word into our lives and by doing things to
help us. We bless God by praising and serving him.

257

September

September 1

Happy is everyone who fears the Lord,
who walks in his ways.
You shall eat the fruit of the labor of your hands;
you shall be happy, and it shall go well with you.

Psalm 128:1–2

Thank you for meaningful, enjoyable work, eternal Father. Thank you for work that provides for the needs I have. Thank you for work that helps others. Thank you for work that contributes to the well-being of society. Thank you that, in all kinds of circumstances, I can work joyfully as unto you and bring honor to your name. Let your blessings be on all the work I do, and may diligence, excellence, and productivity mark the work of my hands. For your glory, I pray. Amen.

On the heels of a job well done come the blessings of a lingering sense of satisfaction and a good night's sleep.

September 2

Let the favor of the Lord our God be upon us,
and prosper for us the work of our hands—
O prosper the work of our hands!

Psalm 90:17

Lord God, today
I offer up to
you as a thank offering
the work you've given
me to do and the ability
you've given me to do
it. I pray that you would
always grant me work
to which I am suited and that when you put in my
hands something that seems beyond my strength
or abilities, I would look to you for what I need and
trust in your grace and power to work through me.
I ask that you would cause what I do to be blessed by
you and, in turn, to be a blessing to others. Thank
you, Lord. Your goodness to me never fails.

Blessed is he who has found his work;
let him ask no other blessedness.

—Thomas Carlyle, *Past and Present*

September 3

Heavenly Father, as grateful as I am for the honorable work you've given me to do, for the ability to earn a living, I confess that I grow weary at times of the long days and the unpleasant parts of my job. I have worked enough to know that there is no job that does not have some element of drudgery or difficulty. So please show me how these parts of my day can become opportunities to become more like your Son, who willingly shouldered a heavy cross to complete the most difficult part of his earthly ministry. By this, he has brought forth the gift of eternal life. May I learn from his example and willingly shoulder my work, knowing that you are working something good in me through it.

Looking to Jesus the pioneer and perfecter of our faith, . . . that you may not grow weary or lose heart.

—Hebrews 12:2–3

261

September 4

Riches I heed not, nor man's empty
praise,
Thou mine Inheritance now and always;
Thou and Thou only first in my heart,
High King of heaven, my Treasure thou art.
High King of heaven, my victory won,
May I reach heaven's joys, O bright heaven's
Sun!
Heart of my own heart, whatever befall,
Still be my Vision, O Ruler of all.

—"Be Thou My Vision," an Irish hymn

In seeking only God, we always
find what we need.

September 5

For he satisfies the thirsty,
and the hungry he fills with good things.

Psalm 107:9

Even though my physical hunger may be satisfied and my thirst quenched, Lord, my soul still has pangs that no meal can satisfy. I admit that I sometimes try to quiet these spiritual "hunger pangs" with temporal things. But it never works when I seek out distractions like eating, buying new stuff, or immersing myself in some form of entertainment. These always pass, leaving me with the sense of need for "something more." O Lord! You are that something more I need. Only you can satisfy this hunger and thirst that nothing else is able to touch. I come to you today, hungry and thirsty for you.

Jesus said to her, "Everyone who drinks of this water will thirst again, but those who drink of the water that I will give them will never be thirsty. The water that I will give will become in them a spring of water gushing up to eternal life."

—John 4:13–14

September 6

*It is in vain that you rise up early
and go late to rest,
eating the bread of anxious toil;
for he gives sleep to his beloved.*

Psalm 127:2

Dear Lord, too often I can go to extremes—rigors you never intend for me—in my attempts to make my ends meet or to secure my position in this life. It's painfully ironic that at these times I am most prone to put off praying and seeking meaningful

fellowship with you. Forgive me for defaulting to self-reliance, for thinking that it's all up to me. Help me trust you so much that I will turn my back on worry and anxiety and, instead, spend time with you, get the rest I need, and allow you to be my source of strength and wisdom.

Sometimes getting a good night's sleep is the most God-honoring thing we can do.

September 7

From the rising of the sun to its setting
the name of the Lord is to be praised.

Psalm 113:3

Today I will praise you, Lord God. I will leave off my concerns and focus on the many reasons I have to give you thanks and praise. Please fill me with a spirit of worship today. May it even overflow to inspire those around me to see and acknowledge how good and wonderful you are.

We were made to turn our hearts to gratitude and joy, not to complaint and despair. And since God is the author of all good and perfect gifts, it is logical that he should be the object of our praise and the recipient of our thanks.

265

September 8

*The fear of the Lord is the beginning of wisdom;
all those who practice it have a good understanding.*

Psalm 111:10

reat and glorious God, I live in a culture
where mocking and disrespect are the
norm, even considered a form of humor. How can
I begin to understand what it means to fear you and
to have reverence and awe for you? O Lord, teach

me what this kind of fear is
and what it means in attitude
and action. I want to learn
your wisdom. The wisdom
of the world is shallow and
can easily collapse, but your
wisdom is timeless, irrefutable,
a safeguard, and a blessing.
Please open my heart and
mind more and more to your
thoughts and ways.

It is only when men begin to worship
that they begin to grow.

—Calvin Coolidge

266

September 9

It is well with those who deal generously and lend,
who conduct their affairs with justice.

Psalm 112:5

Sweetest Lord, make me appreciative of the dignity of my high vocation, and its many responsibilities. Never permit me to disgrace it by giving way to coldness, unkindness, or impatience.

—Mother Teresa, *A Gift for God*

The presence of a gracious soul is like a heaven-sent breeze blowing through a stale room, bringing refreshment and the reminder that there are things in life far superior to one's own interests.

September 10

For the righteous will never be moved. . . .
They are not afraid of evil tidings;
their hearts are firm, secure in the Lord.

Psalm 112:6–7

ear might rise up temporarily in my heart, my Lord, but it can't camp there, not when I keep in mind that my future is everlastingly secure with you. Even death is not an end for me; it is the portal through which I'll pass on the way to my true home in your presence. Anything else

along my path on earth is not to be feared, because you are taking me on my journey to that eternal place of rest and delight.

Even the worst news on earth cannot eclipse the good news of the gospel, which declares God's love and saving grace.

September 11

The Lord has been mindful of us . . .
he will bless those who fear the Lord,
both small and great.

Psalm 115:12–13

*M*ay the road rise to meet you,
May the wind be always at your back,
May the sun shine warm upon your face,
May the rain fall soft upon your fields,
And until we meet again,
May God hold you in the palm of His hand.

—author unknown, "An Irish Wish"

The hope that God will bless us is not a
vain wish; it is a certainty that he who
made us will also be good to us as
we entrust ourselves to his care.

September 12

I kept my faith, even when I said,
"I am greatly afflicted."

Psalm 116:10

*L*ord, I don't understand my suffering, but I will choose to trust you anyway. You are my strength and deliverer. I praise you with all my heart.

I asked God for strength, that I might achieve . . .
I was made weak, that I might learn humbly to obey.
I asked for health, that I might do greater things . . .
I was given infirmity, that I might do better things.
I asked for riches, that I might be happy . . .
I was given poverty, that I might be wise.
I asked for power, that I might have the praise of men . . .
I was given weakness, that I might feel the need of God.
I asked for all things, that I might enjoy life . . .
I was given life, that I might enjoy all things.
I got nothing that I asked for—but everything I had hoped for.
Almost despite myself, my unspoken prayers were answered.
I am, among all men, most richly blessed.

—author unknown, "A Creed for Those Who Have Suffered"

September 13

Out of my distress I called on the Lord;
the Lord answered me and set me in a broad place.

Psalm 118:5

*I*t's just a matter of time, sovereign Lord, until each struggle I face passes and I emerge from a place of distress into a place of deliverance and rest. Help me to never abandon hope in the middle of a trial. May I always press on in prayer, calling out to you, knowing that you hear me and that you are orchestrating the outcome for my eternal good. Hear my prayer even now, for I am calling on you for the deliverance I need this day.

More things are wrought by prayer
than this world dreams of.

—Alfred Lord Tennyson, *The Passing of Arthur*

271

September 14

Return, O my soul, to your rest;
for the Lord has dealt bountifully with you.

Psalm 116:7

*D*ear Lord, you know that my mind, at times, can be like a restless bird flitting about from one thing to the next, trying to manage everything on my agenda. My thoughts of you, however, are like a safe and secure perch on which I can rest, catch my breath, and remember that you are in control and I don't need to be. Remind me of all the times everything has worked out in the end and of how so much of my fluttering and flailing has been wasted energy. Help me not make the mistake of leaving this perch and missing out on all the peaceful ways you work things out for the best for me.

Be devoted to prayer and to listening to God, and he will show you efficiencies and provisions for accomplishing your tasks, ones you never dreamed existed. They will come "out of nowhere" at times, and your amazement and relief will quickly turn into joy and gratitude.

September 15

With the Lord on my side I do not fear.
What can mortals do to me?

Psalm 118:6

*S*ometimes I let the fear of what someone thinks of me or what they might do to me wreak havoc on my peace of mind, most holy Father. You know this is so; you've seen me fret and stew about such things. I want to remember today that even though someone else might be bigger or more powerful than I am—or they might just be downright mean-spirited—whatever the case, you are greater than they are and able to shelter me from the harm of their threats or assaults. I don't want to be afraid anymore, and with you by my side I don't need to be. Thank you, Lord.

People may harm me, even kill me, but they cannot destroy me, for God has made me his child. That is to say, through Christ, he has made me immortal.

September 16

*It is better to take refuge in the Lord
than to put confidence in mortals.*

Psalm 118:8

Who do I call first in a crisis? Is it you, my Lord? I know it's not bad to call on others to support me when I'm in trouble or struggling in some way, but people are limited in their understanding, wisdom, power, and resources, and you are not. Help me "practice" seeking refuge in you in the everyday challenges of life, so I'll be in the habit of calling on you when the more startling and troubling events occur. There is no one else I'd rather have as a support and refuge, dear Lord, than you.

People limp through life, each leaning upon someone else. What, then, if one should stumble and fall? They would go down like dominoes. But mark the wise who keep their eyes fixed ahead on God, who seems beyond but who actually makes them stand strong by his power within them.

September 17

The Lord is my strength and my might;
he has become my salvation.

Psalm 118:14

ear Lord, there's this notion that we are supposed to improve ourselves—that is, be more able to support ourselves and "carry our own weight." But I'm not convinced that my own strength is of any benefit to me. When I seem to have a lot of it, I grow independent of you; but when I feel weak, I stay close to you and am carried along by your strength. I'm beginning to believe my biggest strength is my weakness—that is, the realization of my great need for you.

[The Lord] said to me, "My grace is sufficient for you, for power is made perfect in weakness." So, I will boast all the more gladly of my weaknesses, so that the power of Christ may dwell in me.

—2 Corinthians 12:9

September 18

Nevertheless I am continually with you;
you hold my right hand.
You guide me with your counsel,
and afterward you will receive me with honor.

Psalm 73:23–24

I went to sleep last night with you reminding me of your love, dear Lord. I awoke this morning knowing you were with me. Your presence is my comfort at all times and in all things. To know that I never will be parted from you is my greatest gift in life.

Nothing—not anything—can separate us from the Lord, our God.

September 19

I treasure your word in my heart,
so that I may not sin against you.

Psalm 119:11

To take in a bit of your Word each day, my supreme Lord, is to feed my soul and spirit. Even a small morsel of truth from you can be multiplied throughout my day like the loaves and the fishes were after Jesus' seaside sermon. And when I "chew" on a passage of Scripture, it not only nourishes my faith but also strengthens my resistance to temptation. Thank you for the precious resource of your Word that reminds me of and keeps me safe in your will.

It has been said of the Bible: "This book will keep me from sin, or sin will keep me from this book."

September 20

There was a time in my life when I tried to read your Word, and it just didn't mean that much to me because I didn't understand it.  But Lord, the longer I've walked with you, the more precious, meaningful, and essential the Scriptures have become to me. Thank you for giving me the comprehension to perceive your truth. Please continue to open my understanding to the things of your Spirit—the things written in your Word—that I may walk even more closely with you.

Just as our Lord was able and willing to restore physical eyesight to the blind as he ministered on earth, so he is able to grant spiritual sight to those who seek him.

September 21

Before I was humbled I went astray,
but now I keep your word.

Psalm 119:67

Teach me, O God, so to use all the circumstances of my life today that they may bring forth in me the fruits of holiness rather than the fruits of sin. Let me use disappointment as material for patience. Let me use success as material for thankfulness. Let me use trouble as material for perseverance. Let me use danger as material for courage. Let me use reproach as material for long suffering. Let me use praise as material for humility. Let me use pleasures as material for temperance. Let me use pain as material for endurance.

—John Baillie, *A Diary of Private Prayer*

It is said that a shepherd will break the leg of a sheep that consistently exposes itself to danger by straying off. As the lamb heals from this painful remedy, it learns to depend on the shepherd, who binds up the lamb's brokenness, then carries it on his shoulders, and finally guides it into safe pastures, where the lamb walks close to him.

September 22

I will never forget your precepts,
for by them you have given me life.

Psalm 119:93

My own ways and the ways of the world have brought grief into my life and into the lives of people I love, heavenly Father. To follow such ways is to die a slow spiritual death. Thank you for intervening in my life and for putting my feet on your path. I don't know where I'd be

today if you hadn't rescued me; I don't want to imagine it. I just want to continue following you. Keep me, I pray, in your life-giving ways all my days.

A precept is a command or a principle for living life. God's precepts are intended for us to live righteously and selflessly.

September 23

*D*ear Lord, if it weren't for your Word, my attempts to find my way in life would look like a dizzy person trying to find his or her way, blindfolded. I can think of no better

description. Thankfully, by your Word, I can discover your wisdom for navigating through life, which is so often opposite to my natural inclinations. I'm grateful that you light my way today by what has been written.

God considers human reason, wisdom, morality, and even sunlight, for that matter, to be dark and hazy compared to his Word. God's Word is a flame that shines in the darkness.... If we use this light, then God will no longer remain hidden from us.

—Martin Luther, *Faith Alone: A Daily Devotional*

September 24

I wait for the Lord, my soul waits,
and in his word I hope.

Psalm 130:5

The promises in your Word, Lord, are the promises I cling to. Sometimes when I hear the often-quoted ones, however, my familiarity puts me in danger of seeing them as clichés. O God, forgive me for the times I've done this! May your promises always be precious to me and my hope in

them remain alive. Help me to not brush past the truth but to wonder at your Word, no matter how many times I hear or read it.

Scripture is never irrelevant to our lives, and there is always something new to discover. It only takes slowing down, pausing to look, and waiting to see. Then, in that humble expectation, we are shown what we never saw before, though we'd passed that way a thousand times before.

September 25

Gladden the soul of your servant,
for to you, O Lord, I lift up my soul.

Psalm 86:4

Autumn has arrived, Lord God, and winter is not far off. Days of cold and waiting lie ahead. So please go before me and lead me forward with a glad heart. Let me begin today by lifting up my soul to you to be made glad, not by my circumstances, but by my relationship with you, and just by the fact that you have made me and you love me. Satisfy my heart, dear Lord, and make my soul glad.

To be glad to wake, to be glad to serve, to be glad to work, to be glad to eat, to be glad to love, and to be glad to sleep is to be glad to live and to live indeed!

September 26

Set a guard over my mouth, O Lord,
keep watch over the door of my lips.

Psalm 141:3

Dear Lord, I have many regrets: a bit of gossip, a curse, a mocking tone, a complaint, a sarcastic reply, a put-down, a cruel retort, and a cold greeting. How much damage a selfish attitude and an uncontrolled tongue can do in just a moment's time! Please forgive me, and please heal the wounds I've inflicted, and if possible, allow me to participate in that healing process. Restore the relationships I've damaged and reveal to me how I can make humble amends. Help me today, almighty God, with this new opportunity to speak well of others and kindly to them, to be an encourager and comforter, a peacemaker and a blessing. For your name's sake, I pray.

There is always time to add a word,
never to withdraw one.

—Baltasar Gracian, *The Art of Worldly Wisdom*

September 27

Teach me to do your will,
for you are my God.
Let your good spirit lead me
on a level path.

Psalm 143:10

O gracious and holy Father, give us wisdom to perceive Thee, intelligence to understand Thee, diligence to seek Thee, patience to wait for Thee, eyes to behold Thee, a heart to  meditate upon Thee, and a life to proclaim Thee; through the power of the Spirit of Jesus Christ our Lord.

—Attributed to St. Benedict of Nursia

I say I want the will of God until his will crosses my own. Then I do not want his will at all, but the vital question is not one of desiring but of doing. Will I do his will even when my own is in opposition to it? By God's Spirit I can be made willing and able.

September 28

The Lord upholds all who are falling,
and raises up all who are bowed down.

Psalm 145:14

O Lord! Thou knowest how busy I must be
this day: if I forget thee, do not thou
forget me.

—Sir Jacob Astley

The prayer above was uttered by a soldier before a
battle in the English Civil War. Some of our days on
earth can be like a series of little wars on many fronts.
How consumed we can become by them, by the energy
and attention they require of us! If we forget God in
the heat of battle, however, he does not forget us.
And when we become mindful again of our need
for him, he is just as near as he was the last
time we were fully aware of his presence.

September 29

He fulfills the desire of all who fear him;
he also hears their cry, and saves them.

Psalm 145:19

My Lord, I desire that your kingdom come to flourish in the hearts of those who seek you and that your will be carried out here on earth in the way it is carried out in heaven. I desire enough provision for today's needs. I desire to abide in your strength that I might not give way to temptation. I desire to have a heart of forgiveness like your own that I may extend to others the kind of forgiveness I so desperately need from you. I desire to honor and glorify you all the days of my life and into eternity. Please save me from anything that would thwart and hinder these desires from being fulfilled by you. In your name, I pray. Amen.

The closer we get to God, the more our desires resemble his own. Those who fear God, who revere and honor him, are not focused on gratifying themselves. That is why God can fulfill their desires without compromising his own character.

September 30

The Lord will fulfill his purpose for me.
Psalm 138:8

*F*ather in heaven, in my younger days I wanted you to fulfill *my* purposes. I wanted you to adopt my plans as your own for my life, as if I could order you around and have you serve my selfish purposes. Now those thoughts and attitudes embarrass me. But over time, you have gently and graciously revealed that flaw of foolishness in my understanding and have helped me see that you created me a certain way to fulfill the tailor-made purpose you have for my life. It is a purpose that will fulfill and bless me as well as be a blessing to others. And best of all, it brings honor to your name when people see that you're the one who has brought about such good things in my life.

"For surely I know the plans I have for you," says the Lord, "plans for your welfare and not for harm, to give you a future with hope."

—Jeremiah 29:11

October

October 1

For he did not despise or abhor
the affliction of the afflicted;
he did not hide his face from me,
but heard when I cried to him.

Psalm 22:24

Dear Lord, I'm grateful for your compassion and mercy. When I'm in need, you don't scold or lecture, but you welcome me with open arms. Please fill my heart with that kind of love, so I can do the same for others. Often I run away from people in need, fearing some entanglement and worried that they'll need more than I can give. Or I judge them, assuming they've brought their problems on themselves. Give me the sense of mercy that pushes past those obstacles and help me truly love others in your name.

"Lord, when was it that we saw you hungry and gave you food, or thirsty and gave you something to drink? . . . " And the king will answer them, "Truly I tell you, just as you did it to one of the least of these who are members of my family, you did it to me."

—Matthew 25:37, 40

October 2

Our steps are made firm by the Lord,
when he delights in our way;
though we stumble, we shall not fall headlong,
for the Lord holds us by the hand.

Psalm 37:23–24

Step by step you help me go.
Step by step I learn and grow.
Step by step you guide me well.
Step by—oops, I nearly fell.
Step by step you take delight
To pick me up and make things right.
Step by step and hand in hand
With you, along the path you've planned.

Since we live by the Spirit,
let us keep in step with the Spirit.

—Galatians 5:25 (NIV)

October 3

The heavens are the work of your hands.
They will perish, but you endure;
they will all wear out like a garment.
You change them like clothing, and they pass away;
but you are the same, and your years have no end.

Psalm 102:25–27

oly Creator God, I look at an ocean and I marvel. I see a mountain and I say, "That's something!" The sheer magnitude of that bit of creation is awesome to me. I see a canyon cut by a river and I delight in your artistry. But what is truly amazing is that you outlast all of these majestic masterpieces. I gaze at the night sky with its untold stars, and I exult in the wonder of your creation, but I don't worship what you've made. I bow only before you, the Creator.

Have you not known? Have you not heard?
The Lord is the everlasting God,
the Creator of the ends of the earth.
He does not faint or grow weary;
his understanding is unsearchable.

—Isaiah 40:28

October 4

Happy are those who observe justice,
who do righteousness at all times.

Psalm 106:3

y Lord, I don't always know the right thing to do, but I try. Sometimes the injustice in my world is simply overwhelming. I don't know where to start. Help me treat people justly, putting aside any prejudices I might harbor. Give me courage to point out injustice where I see it and to speak up when necessary, even if that makes me unpopular. So often I get wrapped up in my own concerns. Open my eyes to see where others aren't getting a fair shake.

Learn to do good;
seek justice,
rescue the oppressed,
defend the orphan,
plead for the widow.

—Isaiah 1:17

October 5

Praise him for his mighty deeds;
praise him according to his surpassing greatness!

Psalm 150:2

Creating the universe. Making human beings. Showing mercy to the murderer Cain. Flooding the earth but saving Noah's family. Speaking to Abraham and leading him. Wrestling with Jacob. Guiding Joseph from pit to prison to palace. Parting the Red Sea. Giving the Law. Toppling Jericho's walls. Stopping the sun in its tracks. Empowering a shepherd boy to fell a giant. Burning Elijah's wet sacrifice. Carrying your people back from captivity. Empowering Esther. Taming Daniel's lions. Coming to earth as a baby.... These are just some of the mighty deeds I praise you for, O Lord. And I haven't even started on the things you've done for me in my life.

> Trust in him, ye saints, forever.
> He is faithful, changing never.
> Neither force nor guile can sever
> Those he loves from him.
>
> —Thomas Kelly, "Praise the Savior,
> ye who know him"

October 6

The Lord is my strength and my shield;
in him my heart trusts;
so I am helped, and my heart exults,
and with my song I give thanks to him.

Psalm 28:7

*I*t is in you, my Lord, that we are made holy, righteous, and set apart for service to you. Thank you for taking the initiative to make saints of sinners. And when I think of you delighting in me, I delight in the thought of it. What does your delight look like, I wonder? Mine is full of gratitude toward you, and I cannot wait for the day when we can delight in one another face to face. Until then, it is indeed a noble distinction to belong to you.

With thankful hearts, O Lord, we come
To praise thy name in grateful song.
Accept the offering, Lord, we bring,
And help us loud thy praises sing.

—J. S. Mohler

October 7

Search me, O God, and know my heart;
test me and know my thoughts.
See if there is any wicked way in me,
and lead me in the way everlasting.

Psalm 139:23–24

Dear Lord, I want to please you inside and out. I don't want to be like those Pharisees who prided themselves on clean living but had greedy hearts. I want to be motivated by your desires. Let me put away pride and even religious pride. Help me set aside self-centeredness. I want to take pleasure in your pleasure. Scour my heart so it sparkles before your holy gaze.

Woe to you, scribes and Pharisees, hypocrites! For you clean the outside of the cup and of the plate, but inside they are full of greed and self-indulgence.... First clean the inside of the cup, so that the outside also may become clean.

—Matthew 23:25–26

October 8

O Lord, I love the house in which you dwell,
and the place where your glory abides.

Psalm 26:8

Reading this verse, heavenly Father, I immediately think of church buildings, and I rejoice in the wonderful moments I've had in the gathering of believers. But then I realize that this is not your only dwelling. I'm sure the psalmist was thinking of the tabernacle or temple, but the New Testament announces that my body is a temple of the Holy Spirit. Your glory abides in me! So I'll still savor the time spent in your presence with the community of faith, but I also love the hours we share together, you and I, when you whisper that you are close beside, and even *inside,* me.

Do you not know that your body is a temple of the Holy Spirit within you, which you have from God, and that you are not your own? For you were bought with a price; therefore glorify God in your body.

—1 Corinthians 6:19–20

October 9

Why are you cast down, O my soul,
and why are you disquieted within me?
Hope in God; for I shall again praise him,
my help and my God.

Psalm 42:5–6

As you know, O God, I get downhearted sometimes. Things start going badly, and of course my spirits sag. I love the fact that you remain with me in these troubled times. You understand my emotions because you made them. You've also felt sorrow yourself. I feel that you truly grasp what I'm going through, and that's a comfort to me. This gives me hope. When the tears are spent, when the bad mood has run its course, and when I'm ready to rejoin the human race, I know you'll be right beside me.

My soul is bereft of peace; I have forgotten what happiness is; ... My soul continually thinks of it and is bowed down within me. But this I call to mind, and therefore I have hope: The steadfast love of the Lord never ceases, his mercies never come to an end.

—Lamentations 3:17, 20–22

October 10

*He will redeem me unharmed
from the battle that I wage,
for many are arrayed against me.*

Psalm 55:18

*S*ometimes, when I leave my home, heavenly Father, it feels as if I'm going off to war. Other times, my home itself seems like a battleground. People challenge my decisions, they compete with me, they want this or that from me, they disagree on the silliest things, and they blame me for everything that goes wrong. And things do go wrong! The wounds I sustain each day are substantial, and that's why I come to you today, dear Lord. Please strengthen me. Shield me from destructive criticism. Bolster my feelings against the deflating comments I hear. Give me the confidence I need to do what I'm called to do. I don't need to win this war, my Lord—just survive it.

Do not be overcome by evil, but overcome evil with good.

—Romans 12:21

October 11

I confess my iniquity;
I am sorry for my sin.

Psalm 38:18

What can I say, Lord? I have displeased you again, and I have no good excuse. I knew what was right, and I did what was wrong. I wish I could say it will never happen again, but

I can't. Well, I could *say* that, but we both know it's a constant struggle. Lord, I am truly, deeply sorry— and I'll try to do better. I beg for your forgiveness, and I count on your strength to help me do the right thing in the future.

I do not understand my own actions. For I do not do what I want, but I do the very thing I hate.... Who will rescue me from this body of death? Thanks be to God through Jesus Christ our Lord!

—Romans 7:15, 24–25

October 12

The mighty one, God the Lord,
speaks and summons the earth
from the rising of the sun to its setting.

Psalm 50:1

Almighty God, when you speak, I listen. Why wouldn't I? You are the creator of human life, and I know you are right about how I should live. So keep speaking to me through the Scriptures. Keep nudging me with your Spirit. Bring to my mind those matters you want me to pay attention to. Help me pull away from the TV, the Internet, the cell phone, and the video games, and let me set my focus on you.

In the beginning was the Word, and the Word was with God, and the Word was God. [Jesus] was in the beginning with God. All things came into being through him, and without him not one thing came into being.

—John 1:1–3

October 13

Everlasting God, I know all about rejection. Job applications. Bank loans. "Friends" who suddenly turn their backs. But you are eternally faithful, dear Lord, and I am truly grateful. You're ready to hear my prayers 24/7, and you keep showing me your love in unexpected ways. So today I bring my requests to you for the situations I care about, for my loved ones, and for my own spiritual growth. Lord, please hear my prayers.

Ask, and it will be given you; search, and you will find; knock, and the door will be opened for you. For everyone who asks receives, and everyone who searches finds, and for everyone who knocks, the door will be opened.

—Matthew 7:7–8

October 14

Rain in abundance, O God, you showered abroad;
you restored your heritage when it languished;
your flock found a dwelling in it;
in your goodness, O God, you provided for the needy.

Psalm 68:9–10

O good shepherd, seek me out, and bring me home to thy fold again. Deal favorably with me according to thy good pleasure, till I may dwell in thy house all the days of my life, and praise thee for ever and ever with them that are there.

—Saint Jerome

Rain is a very good thing in the arid climate of the Holy Land. This psalm praises the Lord for sending rain whenever the land of his people needs it.

October 15

There's a highway in my heart, dear Lord, and it heads right to your home. When I need comfort, I go to you. When I need wisdom, I go to you. When I need courage or forgiveness

or creativity, I hop on that highway and head in your direction. You are always there to meet me. Thank you, my Lord, for all you mean to me.

October 16

Be strong, and let your heart take courage,
all you who wait for the Lord.

Psalm 31:24

O for a faith that will not shrink though
      pressed by many a foe,
That will not tremble on the brink of any earthly woe,
That will not murmur nor complain beneath the
      chastening rod,
But in the hour of grief or pain will lean upon its God,
A faith that shines more bright and clear when
      tempests rage without,
That, when in danger, knows no fear, in darkness
      feels no doubt.
Lord, give me such a faith as this, and then,
      whatever may come,
I'll taste even now the hallowed bliss of an eternal home.

—William H. Bathurst

By faith we understand that the worlds
   were prepared by the word of God,
      so that what is seen was made
      from things that are not visible.

—Hebrews 11:3

305

October 17

The idols of the nations are silver and gold,
the work of human hands.
They have mouths, but they do not speak;
they have eyes, but they do not see; . . .
Those who make them
and all who trust them
shall become like them.

Psalm 135:15–16, 18

My Lord, idols come in many flawed forms. They may be a celebrity, a dream job, a big house, or even an unhealthy relationship. If this is true with me, reveal that idol to me, humble my pride, and draw me close to you. Lord, only you are worthy of my worship. Please forgive my wandering heart and embrace me once again. I want to worship only you.

You shall love the Lord your God with all your heart, and with all your soul, and with all your might.

—Deuteronomy 6:5

October 18

You will not fear the terror of the night,
or the arrow that flies by day,
or the pestilence that stalks in darkness,
or the destruction that wastes at noonday.

Psalm 91:5–6

O Lord, I see terror all around me. People are afraid to travel, afraid to invest, and afraid even to step outside. The world is a powder keg, the economy is iffy, and I never know if I'm coming down with the flu or some dread disease. Yet you tell me I don't need to be afraid, and I'll take you at your word. Whatever might happen to my world or to me, I know that you will be with me. I find great comfort in that assurance. Give me the ability to comfort others with that same truth.

Terror thrives on uncertainty. While we may not know what the future holds, we certainly know who holds the future.

October 19

Worship the Lord in holy splendor;
tremble before him, all the earth.

Psalm 96:9

Today, dear Lord, I worship you with all that I am and all that I have. Whatever creative gifts I have, I offer them to you—songs, words, movement, and color. You are a great God, my support and my redeemer. You have shown me your love in countless ways, and I love you in return. You never cease to amaze me with your kindness and wisdom. I praise you today, and I'll praise you tomorrow. I owe everything to you.

Before the Lord, everyone is an artist. The worshipful expression of a God-given imagination is beautiful to behold!

October 20

Make a joyful noise to the Lord, all the earth.
Worship the Lord with gladness;
come into his presence with singing.

Psalm 100:1–2

*S*ing praise to God who reigns above,
    the God of all creation,
The God of power, the God of love, the God of our
    salvation.
With healing balm my soul he fills
    and every faithless murmur stills
To God all praise and glory.
What God's almighty power has made, his gracious
    mercy keeps.
By morning glow or evening shade his watchful eye
    never sleeps.
Within the kingdom of his might,
    all is just and all is right.
To God all praise and glory.

—Johann J. Schutz

Why do we get passionately bothered about the
styles of worship we don't like? Worship isn't
for us. It's an offering we give to God.

October 21

The voice of the Lord is over the waters;
the God of glory thunders,
the Lord, over mighty waters.

Psalm 29:3

The thunder rolls, supreme and all-powerful God, and I think of your mighty voice speaking light into darkness. The lightning flashes, and I also think of those flashes of insight you give us—moments when we see things from your perspective and know what we need to do. Awesome Lord, I ask you to thunder into my life. Bring light into my darkness and love into my indifference. Give me flashes of clarity to know how to serve you most effectively in this challenging world.

Thunderstorms can be terrifying, as well as energizing. Filling our world with sound and light, it's an awesome display. And it's just a hint of the nature of our terrifying and energizing God.

October 22

With my mouth I will give great thanks to the Lord;
I will praise him in the midst of the throng.
For he stands at the right hand of the needy,
to save them from those who would condemn them to death.

Psalm 109:30–31

*S*how me where to stand, gracious Lord. If you stand at the right hand of the needy, I want to be there too. What can I do to help? Soften my heart and sharpen my eyes so I notice the needs

around me and feel the urge to assist. I know I can't solve everyone's problems, but I want to reach out with your love and power to make life a little better for someone who's hurting. Please show me the way.

Has not God chosen the poor in the world to be rich in faith and to be heirs of the kingdom that he has promised to those who love him?

—James 2:5

October 23

I will come praising the mighty deeds of the Lord God,
I will praise your righteousness, yours alone.

Psalm 71:16

Holy God, I ask for your righteousness to fill me, thrill me, captivate me, and motivate me. I want a righteousness steeped in your love rather than in my own pride. I want a righteous

life that emanates a deep sense of gratitude and not a holier-than-thou attitude. This isn't about me being some sort of spiritual giant. It's about you living your life through me. In Jesus' sacred name, I pray. Amen.

We don't find righteousness in good behavior.
We find good behavior by relying on
the righteousness of Christ.

October 24

I can almost
feel the earth
tottering, O God. It's
good to know you keep a
tight grip on those pillars.
Seriously, I worry about
what we've done to this
planet—polluted air,

tainted water, depleted ozone, and melted glaciers.
I know you care about the earth too, so I ask you
to help me take good care of it. Show me how to
protect your creation without worshipping it. Teach
me to be a good steward of what you have given us.

313

October 25

For who in the skies can be compared to the Lord?
Who among the heavenly beings is like the Lord?

Psalm 89:6

You don't pull punches, do you, heavenly Father? You don't shy away from challenges. The psalmist asks the other nations to put their gods up against you, and there's no contest. No one compares to you. But all of this makes me think about how I relate to those with other beliefs. Should I engage in "trash talk," insisting my faith is better than theirs? Not if I want to show your love. So please, Lord, help me speak the truth in love, being both wise and caring, while being honest about my faith but respectful of others.

Always be ready to make your defense to anyone who demands from you an accounting for the hope that is in you; yet do it with gentleness and reverence.

—1 Peter 3:15–16

October 26

O magnify the Lord with me,
and let us exalt his name together.

Psalm 34:3

*D*ear Lord, I can talk with my friends about anything and everything—traffic, children, weather, TV, and sports—you name it. But it's harder to talk about you. Why is that? Lord, it should be the most natural thing in the world to share what you're doing in my life and to hear similar reports from others. Help me open up about you, so my friends and I can magnify you together.

You are the light of the world. A city built on a hill cannot be hid. No one after lighting a lamp puts it under the bushel basket, but on the lampstand, and it gives light to all in the house. In the same way, let your light shine before others.

—Matthew 5:14–16

October 27

For you, O Lord, have made me glad by your work;
at the works of your hands I sing for joy.

Psalm 92:4

I rejoice today, O brilliant Creator, in the glory of what you have made. The sheer majesty of mountains and oceans is awe-inspiring, not to mention planets and galaxies. But it's just as inspiring if I turn my gaze to the tiniest parts of your creation—an insect's body armor, a plant's growth process, and a strand of human DNA. You have made everything with wit and wonder, including me! I am privileged to be called your child.

People quibble about the *process* of creation, but it's the *purpose* that's actually important.

October 28

Dear Lord, as you know, I've had some difficult times. On a number of occasions in my life I have felt totally lost. I've had no idea what to do. I've been emotionally wounded by people I expected to treat me better. I have suffered grave disappointments. But as I think back over those times, my heart is filled with gratitude, because I cried out to you and you helped me. You transformed some of those situations, but you also transformed me. So I thank you from the core of who I am today. Where would I be without you? *Who* would I be? I owe my entire existence to you.

He is the living God, enduring forever. His kingdom shall never be destroyed, and his dominion has no end. He delivers and rescues, he works signs and wonders in heaven and on earth.

—Daniel 6:26–27

October 29

O my Father in heaven, I love doing your work. It's a great feeling to be filled with your strength, to use the abilities you have given me, and to accomplish something in your name. This isn't about earning a special place at your table. I'm not trying to win an extra heavenly crown so I can parade around the golden streets in style. No, I count it a privilege to serve you. I realize that it's only through your power that I accomplish anything. So the only crown I need is your smile. To know that you are pleased with my effort—that makes it all worthwhile.

God works and we work.

—Medieval monastic saying

October 30

Your decrees are very sure;
holiness befits your house,
O Lord, forevermore.

Psalm 93:5

*D*oes holiness befit *my* house, righteous Lord? As I think about the activities that go on in my home, the attitudes displayed, and the priorities represented, is it a holy place? I hope so. That's my desire. Do we put more emphasis on loving you than in acquiring electronic gadgets? Do we love each other rather than fight all the time? Is honesty a hallmark of this home, or do we sneak and hide and deceive and manipulate? Dear Lord, I want a holy home. That's why I dedicate my dwelling place to you. I want *you* to feel at home here.

Home is where the heart is most fully what it is.

319

October 31

Even though I walk through the darkest valley,
I fear no evil;
for you are with me;
your rod and your staff—
they comfort me.

Psalm 23:4

The sidewalks are filled today with goblins, or at least ghoulish costumes. Like it or not, many play at being scary. But there have been genuinely scary times in my life, when I had to face real danger and when I truly fretted about the outcome. I've had to walk through some "dark valleys" of disease, disaster, and desertion. In such times, each step becomes an act of great courage. Lord, you have found ways to comfort me in those difficult periods. You have assured me that you are

 right beside me, helping me to take each new step. So how can I be terrified when you are my protector?

Cast all your anxiety on him,
because he cares for you.

—1 Peter 5:7

November

November 1

You crown the year with your bounty.

Psalm 65:11

By your grace, heavenly Father, another harvest has been gathered in—all those grains, fruits, and vegetables to sustain our lives, just as harvests have done from time immemorial. And now comes the time of our gathering together as friends and family to celebrate. As I move into this season of thanksgiving and celebration, my great God, help me keep a light heart, remembering your goodness and praising you for your provisions, both physical and spiritual.

Season of mists and mellow fruitfulness,
Close bosom-friend of the maturing sun;
Conspiring with him how to load and bless
With fruit the vines that round the thatch-eaves run.

—John Keats, "To Autumn"

November 2

I will give thanks to the Lord with my whole heart;
I will tell of all your wonderful deeds.

Psalm 9:1

What would it look like for me to give you thanks with my whole heart, Lord? I want to offer a thank offering like that to you, one that I am excited to give and that comes from the bottom of my heart. Please stir my heart toward that end, and as you open up the wellspring of gratitude in my heart, I will meditate on and talk about all the ways you have blessed me from the earliest years of my life right up to this present moment.

Gratitude has eyes to see the subtlest shade of blessing, the ability to feel even the gentlest touch of God's goodness.

323

November 3

I will praise the name of God with a song;
I will magnify him with thanksgiving.

Psalm 69:30

eavenly Father, it is almost the end of the year. I had determined at the beginning of the year to be glad in you and to regularly sing out my praises to you. Now the season of thanksgiving is upon us, and I want to recommit to singing my praises to you. I want to think of a love

song I can sing to you or a hymn or maybe a worship chorus. Singing to you helps me draw near you like no other form of prayer. Thank you for the gift of music!

To worship in song is to bring a bit of heaven into our homes ... not because of our singing ability, but because a worshipful spirit set to music transcends what is earthly and joins itself with what is heavenly.

November 4

Sing aloud to God our strength;
shout for joy to the God of Jacob.

Psalm 81:1

*A*ll of what I call "my strengths" are from you, dear Lord. You are the source of all strength, and I am dependent on you each day for everything. But instead of acknowledging you for these things as a duty, please help me rejoice in you because of them. I want to know thankfulness as a delight or thrill at your goodness to me. I want to be so happy in you and so thankful for your generous gifts that I always feel compelled to point out your goodness without hesitation or to share the wonder of your ways with someone nearby—a friend, a family member, a coworker. I want to be a child who "shouts" and sings for joy because of you, O God, my strength and provider.

Do you have eyesight? It's a gift. Do you have a good mind? It's a gift. How about dexterity in your fingers? Or special skills that allow you to work in your occupation?...These are all gifts from God's hand. Reflect on His numerous gifts to you. It will increase your joy. It will make you smile!

—Chuck Swindoll, *Great Attitudes!*

November 5

Faithfulness will spring up from the ground,
and righteousness will look down from the sky.

Psalm 85:11

*W*hen you preside over hearts, homes, and nations, Lord, your ways become established, your ways of faithfulness and righteousness. I know there are no perfect people, families, or countries, but there are people and places you have made pleasant by your grace at work within them. Please make me one of those people whose presence is a pleasant place for others to be. Reveal your own goodness through my life—your righteousness and faithfulness. In your name, I ask. Amen.

There's a special man at my church. He never fails to show up and help get things ready for the worship service. If he didn't show up, people would be alarmed; he's that faithful. He has some other wonderful character qualities; for example, he's humble—the guy's an M.D. who has discovered cures for diseases—and is as glad to set up coffee pots as he is to go on medical mission trips. The time he's spent in God's hands has made him that way.

November 6

The Lord will give what is good,
and our land will yield its increase.

Psalm 85:12

Almighty Lord, the soil of my soul is daily gathering the seeds of my thoughts, attitudes, and deeds. May your own hands weed the soil and cause only the best to grow as I confess my failings and give you glory for the good you've sown within me.

Jesus said to him, "...No one is good but God alone."

—Mark 10:18

November 7

*I give thanks to you, O Lord my God, with my whole heart,
and I will glorify your name forever.*

Psalm 86:12

Supreme Creator, when good things happen, when I feel your presence, and when my desires are granted, I want to praise you. But when everything in my life seems to be going nowhere or worse, I often fall silent and sometimes even become angry. That's why, heavenly Father, I need to dwell on your goodness. The reality of your blessings never stops, but when my perception of them fails, please remind me of better times and that you are worthy of my praise at all times. That way, I can keep on giving you the glory you richly deserve.

Gratitude is the memory of the heart.

—Jean Baptiste Massieu

November 8

I will sing of your steadfast love, O Lord, forever;
with my mouth I will proclaim your faithfulness to all generations.

Psalm 89:1

While Thanksgiving Day nears, heavenly Father, the young people in my life are happy because they'll get some days off from school and will enjoy festivities, friends, and family. I wonder how many of them are thinking of you and how good you are to them. I would be extremely happy to be able to gently and yet effectively speak a word or hold up a meaningful tradition or do something that would plant a seed of gratitude toward you in their hearts and minds. But if all I can do is pray for them, then I'll gladly do that today with hope that you are at work within them, helping them find their way to knowing you and how good you are.

The youth around us might not understand our faith, but if we live it out in such a way that makes it attractive, at some point, they will likely want to know what makes us so "cool."

November 9

It is good to give thanks to the Lord...
to declare your steadfast love in the morning,
and your faithfulness by night.

Psalm 92:1–2

$\mathcal{M}$ost holy Lord, in the quiet and solitude of a midnight snack (or even of maddening insomnia), I have the opportunity to turn my nocturnal thoughts toward you. Let it be that even this night I will find the comfort of your grace-filled presence and be thankful for the gifts of the day—even of the moment. May I commune with you in a tender-hearted return of blessing for blessing.

Was there ever a sanctuary for prayer as apt as the night itself, or ever a place entirely sanctified by gratitude as the shelter of a home on a stormy night?

November 10

O come, let us worship and bow down,
let us kneel before the Lord, our Maker!

Psalm 95:6

To the King of the ages, immortal, invisible, the only God, be honor and glory forever and ever. Amen.

—1 Timothy 1:17

A bent knee is a form of worship that may or may not be accompanied by a humble heart. I can pray that my heart will be right with God, however, even as I bend the knee. May God grant me the heart of a true worshipper!

November 11

Father in heaven, when I ascribe to you what belongs to you, I come into agreement with what is true about who you are. You *are* glorious! More glorious than the most awe-inspiring sunrise or the wonders of the night sky. You *are* strong, Lord! Stronger than the most powerful ocean currents or the quaking of the earth or the eruption of volcanic mountains. I call out your attributes to my family, point to them when they are evident, wonder at them aloud, and declare them to the next generation. You are amazing, my God! I am full of wonder at your works and your ways.

"Ever notice how...?" is a nonthreatening invitation to converse with others about the Lord.

November 12

Let the redeemed of the Lord say so,
those he redeemed from trouble
and gathered in from the lands,
from the east and from the west,
from the north and from the south.

Psalm 107:2–3

ear Lord God, I rejoice that people from every land and of every nation sing your praises. We are all united in our love for you and in our deep appreciation for having redeemed us and made us your beloved children. Thank you for being our God and heavenly Father. Amen.

We are redeemed in Christ! Such a blessing is why we should be a truly grateful people on the face of the Earth.

November 13

The Lord has done great things for us,
and we rejoiced.

Psalm 126:3

I want to take this minute, my Lord, to recite back to you as many things as I can think of that you have done for me this day, this week, this month, this past year. You *have* done great things for me! May a spirit of rejoicing rise up in me as I fill the air with testimonies of all the miracles, graces, and blessings you've poured out on my life.

Always give thanks to the Lord in the manner you appreciate receiving God's blessings—sincerely, thoughtfully, and with exceeding joy.

November 14

May those who sow in tears
reap with shouts of joy.

Psalm 126:5

Thank you, almighty Father, for the "reaping times" of joy after periods of difficulty, hard work, or sorrow. When the dark times engulf me, please keep my heart faithful to you so that I will not miss the inevitable outcome of restoration and rejoicing. Let my love for you be tempered and matured in the seasons of sorrow so that my joy may be made complete in that love, fully ripened at harvest time.

The best way to show our gratitude to God and the people is to accept everything with joy. A joyful heart is the inevitable result of a heart burning with love.

—Mother Teresa, *A Gift for God*

335

November 15

There are so many ways your salvation comes to me, my Savior. I truly can speak of it from day to day. You have kept me safe from death on my journey to understanding your grace. You save me from bad decisions and mistakes, whether that means rescuing me after making them or keeping me from them in the first place. You protect me in the course of the day, often in ways I don't see, but when I lie down, I feel safe from harm at night because of your presence. Your salvation surrounds me, Lord. May I speak of it whenever and wherever I see or experience it.

To be saved by God is no small thing, not that it is a difficult thing for him, but it is an extremely gracious act on his part. To understand that I don't deserve this gift of salvation is the first step in knowing how to be truly grateful for it.

November 16

Great is the Lord, and greatly to be praised;
his greatness is unsearchable.

Psalm 145:3

*D*ear Lord, I realize that the "unsearchableness" of your greatness isn't intended to discourage my searching for it. So many new things occur to me about your wisdom and greatness whenever I stop to examine the world around me. Part of what makes these discoveries so exciting is that I realize I cannot exhaust them. It doesn't matter how many treasures I dig up about your greatness. If I keep digging, I'll keep finding more. And it's wonderful how you tuck away such wonderful gems in the layers of your creation. I'll keep searching as long as I live. Thank you for disclosing yourself in so many ways, especially the ones that take a little "mining" to uncover.

To examine God's work is to discover more about his greatness, which compels me to praise him even more.

November 17

Praise the Lord!
How good it is to sing praises to our God;
for he is gracious. . . .
He heals the brokenhearted,
and binds up their wounds.

Psalm 147:1, 3

The scars you bear, Lord Jesus, are evidence of your wounds. You carry them in your own body. But let the scars in my own life not remind me of the wounds that made them as much as they remind me of your coming to heal them. Thank you for all the gracious ways you've brought healing to my life—to my soul, my mind, my body, and my emotions. I wouldn't be praying this prayer if it weren't for your healing touch. I praise you in your precious name. Amen.

Healing this side of heaven is a foreshadow of the complete healing that awaits us.

November 18

They shall celebrate the fame of your abundant goodness,
and shall sing aloud of your righteousness.

Psalm 145:7

Mary said, "My soul magnifies the Lord, and my spirit rejoices in God my Savior,...for the Mighty One has done great things for me, and holy is his name. His mercy is for those who fear him from generation to generation. He has shown strength with his arm; he has scattered the proud in the thoughts of their hearts. He has brought down the powerful from their thrones, and lifted up the lowly; he has filled the hungry with good things."

—Luke 1:46–47, 49–53

It is a blessing in itself to celebrate God's goodness. The Bible records a number of the faithful who broke into ecstatic praise when God did good things in their lives: Moses, Miriam, Hannah, David, Mary, Elizabeth, and Paul, as well as other apostles. Go ahead! You're in good company.

339

November 19

Surely the righteous shall give thanks to your name;
the upright shall live in your presence.

Psalm 140:13

Thank you for the righteousness I have in you, Lord Jesus. You have granted me the status of a righteous person in your redemption, and you are transforming me in righteous living as I walk

with you by your Spirit. I give you thanks for these things—these amazing mysteries of your grace of which I am a blessed recipient. To live with you, now and forever, is the crowning glory of this journey. Blessed be your name, Lord Jesus!

We walk daily by faith in Christ's presence until the moment we stand eternally before him, finally able to feast our eyes on his wondrous form.

November 20

Your name, O Lord, endures forever,
your renown, O Lord, throughout all ages.

Psalm 135:13

From the Creation to the Judgment, you will cause your name to be exalted among all the peoples of the earth. I do not even know the names of my relatives three generations ago, but I know your name, you who revealed yourself at the dawn of time to the first man and woman. I worship you today, Great One! I'm humbled when I think of such things as this.

Speaking of fame and renown.... The Bible is still the all-time best-selling book of the ages!

November 21

I give you thanks, O Lord, with my whole heart . . .
for your steadfast love and your faithfulness;
for you have exalted your name and your word
above everything.

Psalm 138:1–2

praise you, almighty God. You are the Creator and Maker of all that is good and holy. I exalt your name and bow before your majesty. Your love for me is indeed wonderful, and your words to me are indeed glorious. I sing your praises with this humble prayer now and forever. Amen.

In a more rapidly changing world than ever, the unchangeableness of God—his faithfulness and his mercy—are precious realities on which we gratefully stand firm.

November 22

*Great are the works of the Lord,
studied by all who delight in them.*

Psalm 111:2

I study my own hand, dear Lord—how it moves, the way the joints are placed, and the way my fingers and thumb work together. How amazing the design! How wise you are! And I could study it in more depth from a textbook, and my wonder would only increase. Thank you for revealing your greatness in so many ways—both to the casual observer and the scholar. We all delight in your knowledge, insight, and power.

To study even a single cell is to know that there is a supreme God.

November 23

For the Lord will vindicate his people,
and have compassion on his servants.

Psalm 135:14

Thank you for your compassion, dear Lord. Thank you that you have seen my predicament and shown your mercy to me. Thank you for vindicating me from my enemy, the devil, by bringing your redemption where he had incited rebellion against you and had introduced slavery to sin. By your compassion you have saved me from my rebellion, and by your mercy you have set me free from my sin. Thank you, Lord! I praise your name forever!

"Free at last, Free at last!
Thank God Almighty, I'm free at last!"

—Negro spiritual often quoted by Martin Luther King
Jr. and engraved on his tombstone

November 24

Enter his gates with thanksgiving,
and his courts with praise.
Give thanks to him, bless his name.

Psalm 100:4

I want to come to you, into your presence,
with praise on my lips right now, my Lord.
How well you deserve it! How sad it would be for me
to sweep aside your many blessings to focus only on

the problems of the day!
I won't do that. Instead,
I'll praise you. There will
be time for addressing the
concerns I have, but I will
set my soul and my lips free
to thank you and to bless
your name.

Gratitude is the most exquisite form of courtesy.

—Jacques Maritain, *Reflections on America*

November 25

Today I will remember that you have given me clothes, shelter, and food. Beyond these things, heavenly Father, I've got running water—and warm water, at that!—electricity, heat, lights, transportation, and telephones. Human fellowship, pets, plants, and music. All that is well in my body, my senses, and my mind. And while that list is not even close to being exhaustive, I never want to forget that you yourself are my greatest joy and my most precious gift. Help me always remember all your benefits. Bless the Lord, O my soul.

Is something insignificant just because it happens every day? If the sun wouldn't shine for ten days, suddenly it would be a great thing when it began shining again. If fire existed only in one place on earth, I think it would be more precious than gold or silver. If there were only one well in the world, I would imagine that a drop of water would be worth more than a thousand dollars.

—Martin Luther, *Faith Alone: A Daily Devotional*

November 26

Let everything that breathes praise the Lord!
Praise the Lord!

Psalm 150:6

To see the things that live and breathe on the earth is to witness your genius, almighty Creator. What a treat to see the strange and wonderful creatures and plant life you've made! How intriguing they are with their special defenses and ways of getting food! How they move and migrate and reproduce.... What a fantastic menagerie! Everything that breathes praises you in its own way, Lord God. Praise the Lord, indeed!

Science still has not been able to discover exactly how a cat is able to purr. And let us not forget that God created both cats and us.

November 27

I will praise the Lord as long as I live;
I will sing praises to my God all my life long.

Psalm 146:2

Even if my ability to utter a sound gives way to silence in my old age, dear Lord, I ask that you would grant me grace to make music to you in my heart and mind and to praise you even when my life is coming to an end. By then I should have a treasure trove of memories of the way you've blessed my life. There will be reasons, I'm sure, to be sad, but I'm hoping I will be long practiced in praise and thanksgiving so that I'll be more prone to see your graces in my situation than the disgraces of decline. Let me praise you today in preparation for those days ahead. Amen.

You can guess the ending of your story with a fair amount of accuracy by the direction you are taking the plot today.

November 28

*How very good and pleasant it is
when kindred live together in unity!*

Psalm 133:1

*I*n this season of family get-togethers, my heavenly Father, I thank you for the good things about my family. And, Lord, where there are family challenges and strife, I pray that you would intervene. Please soften hearts, change minds, grant grace and forgiveness...even miracles! Heal our broken relationships, dear Father, and protect our healthy ones. Let unity ultimately prevail—but not a thin, superficial unity that could break at any moment. Please forge an unbreakable unity within our hearts by your righteousness and peace. In Christ's name, I pray. Amen.

Grace, forgiveness, and love are essential
ingredients for unity among believers.

November 29

May you be blessed by the Lord,
who made heaven and earth.

Psalm 115:15

My Lord, you made heaven and earth. You made them by speaking them into existence. When you created the heavens and the earth, you declared them good. You do all things well. Every blessing from your hand is a good and perfect gift. O, help me hold in gratitude what you give me today! Please keep me from losing what you have given me, and may I be ready to share the bounty of your blessings with those around me. In the name of your precious Son, I pray. Amen.

The real issue in life is not how many blessings we have, but what we do with our blessings. Some people have many blessings and hoard them. Some have few and give everything away.

—Fred Rogers, *The World According to Mister Rogers: Important Things to Remember*

November 30

Happy are the people whose God is the Lord.

Psalm 144:15

I've said it before, and I'll say it again, dear Lord: You are my greatest benefit and blessing. When I think of belonging  to you, I get lost in the amazement of that thought. You have made me glad in your care. You have made me hope in your salvation. You have made me believe in your promises. You have made me to love you because you first loved me. What more could I want?

God has made me his own; he calls me his child; he promises me eternity with him in his heavenly home. I trust in him; we delight in each other. That is what it means to me that God is my Father.

December

December 1

When you are disturbed, do not sin;
ponder it on your beds, and be silent.

Psalm 4:4

Dear Lord, sometimes it's best to be quiet. I've said a lot of words in my life, and some of them I regret. I've been disturbed with various people along the way, and I've given them a piece of my mind. Sometimes I get upset with you, usually when I don't understand what you're doing or why you're doing it. You've never seemed to mind it when people express their frustrations to you. Moses, Elijah, David, and Jeremiah were all intimate with you, even though they barked at you once in a while. And yet, sometimes it's best to be quiet. So let me ponder your actions, Lord, in silence. Be with me in the stillness.

Spirit of God, descend upon my heart.
Wean it from earth, through all its pulses move.
Stoop to my weakness, mighty as thou art,
And make me love thee as I ought to love.

—George Croly

December 2

The boundary lines have fallen for me in pleasant places;
I have a goodly heritage.

Psalm 16:6

Thank you, Lord, for the blessings you have bestowed on me. Thank you for the love of my family and for the "extended family" of my circle of friends. Thank you for the work I do each day, whether I get paid for it or not. Thank you for laughter and music and creativity. Thank you for a world rich with wonder. Thank you for the opportunities you have given me to learn and grow, to care and communicate, and to share with others. I think back on all the "coincidences" that have brought me to the place where I am today, and I'm grateful for your hand in them. Those boundary lines don't just *fall* in pleasant places. You put them there. Thank you.

The faithful will abound with blessings.

—Proverbs 28:20

December 3

All the paths of the Lord are steadfast love and faithfulness,
for those who keep his covenant and his decrees.

Psalm 25:10

*W*hat should I do,
gracious Lord? What
choice should I make? So often I
find myself at a fork in the road, and
I have no clue which option is best.
I try to foresee the outcome. I try to gauge my
priorities. I try to determine which path *you* prefer
for me. And it still seems like a toss-up. Then I
start to worry about the consequences of making
a wrong choice. Will I regret what choices I make
later this year or even tomorrow? Will I miss out on
blessings that you want to give me? I can go crazy
worrying about the choices I make. Nevertheless,
the promise I hear from today's psalm is that your
steadfast love operates in "all the paths." Whichever
road I choose, you are faithful.

When the Spirit of truth comes,
he will guide you into all the truth.

—John 16:13

December 4

You are a hiding place for me;
you preserve me from trouble;
you surround me with glad cries of deliverance.

Psalm 32:7

ear Lord, it's a jungle out there. Everyone's rushing to meet their own needs, oblivious to anyone else's. People can be downright mean. They insult and slander me. Even when people act nice, I always wonder how sincere they are. Are they just waiting for me to slip up? But, Lord, I know I can come to you for genuine support. When life is at its craziest, let me hide in you for a while. Speak peace to me with your Spirit. Surround me with others who know what I'm going through. Heal me and renew my energy.

Hiding is both bad and good in the Bible. Adam and Eve hid from God in the Garden, but Rahab did well to hide the Israelite spies in Jericho. Hiding from God is a major problem, but when we flee from harm by hiding in God, it's truly a blessing!

December 5

*Truly the eye of the Lord is on those who fear him,
on those who hope in his steadfast love.*

Psalm 33:18

When I think of your having your eye on me, I picture a stern teacher warning some misbehaving child. But that's not really the right picture, is it, Lord? Maybe you are more like the mother who watches her child playing in the park. She lets the child play, but she's always mindful of her child. If her child skins a knee or is in danger, Mom swoops in to help. In the same way, your eye is on me, heavenly Father, and I thank you. Then again I think of a loving couple having dinner together. The food hardly gets touched because their eyes are on each other. Could that be the relationship that you and I have—my gaze riveted on you, and your eyes enjoying me?

Then the Lord said, "I have observed the misery of my people who are in Egypt; I have heard their cry on account of their taskmasters. Indeed, I know their sufferings."

—Exodus 3:7

December 6

Bless the Lord, O my soul,
and all that is within me,
bless his holy name.

Psalm 103:1

With my whole being, precious Lord, I exalt your wonderful name. Indeed, whenever I hear your people praise your name, my soul is overwhelmed with joy, for you are a great God, who is both just and merciful in all that you do. I bless your holy name now and forever. Amen.

Love the Lord your God with all your heart, and with all your soul, and with all your mind, and with all your strength.

—Mark 12:30

December 7

*A*lmighty God, when I watch a quality TV show or movie, I marvel at the way the writer weaves everything together. The character faced some problem at the beginning that turns out to be a benefit in the end. The plot unfolds perfectly so that the final resolution is surprising, yet somehow obvious. Sometimes my life is like that too, only you are the author. I'm amazed at your understanding and the way you take different elements of my character, good and bad, and weave them into something eternally valuable. Struggles of my past lead to victories in my future. It's hard to keep up with you moment by moment, but every so often I look back and cry out, "Wow!"

December 8

The Lord protects the simple;
when I was brought low, he saved me.

Psalm 116:6

Simple is "in" now, holy Father. Everywhere I look, people are trimming back their Christmas decorations, being thrifty in their fashion, and downsizing their lifestyle. In fact, living more simply has become a multimillion dollar industry. But when I come before you as a "simple" soul, that's not what I'm talking about. It's not a fad; it's just the stark reality. I have no grand gift to offer. I would love to paint a masterpiece for you, sing the best worship song ever, and feed all the poor people in my county, but I can't. I just bring myself—undecorated, unpackaged, and un-anything—to you.

Blissful are the simple, for they shall have much peace.

—Thomas à Kempis

December 9

And now, O Lord, what do I wait for?
My hope is in you.

Psalm 39:7

*I*n the first two decades of my life, I couldn't wait to get older. It's a world full of waiting, my Lord. People wait for paychecks and bank loans, phone calls from loved ones, tech support, and the end of the working day. What am I waiting for? Sure, I have my dreams of what the future might bring, but I'm beginning to realize that those dreams might disappoint me. But you don't disappoint me, Lord. Ultimately you are the only one worth waiting for. What "better life" could there be than a life spent with you?

For the grace of God has appeared, bringing salvation to all, training us to renounce impiety and worldly passions, and in the present age to live lives that are self-controlled, upright, and godly, while we wait for the blessed hope and the manifestation of the glory of our great God and Savior, Jesus Christ.

—Titus 2:11–13

December 10

You have kept count of my tossings;
put my tears in your bottle.
Are they not in your record?

Psalm 56:8

One of the worst things about my times of
grief and struggle is the feeling that no
one knows and no one cares. I feel all alone in a vast
wilderness. I toss and turn at night, crying myself
to sleep and haunted by a sense of utter loneliness.
But that's not really the case, heavenly Father.
Like a parent keeping a scrapbook of a child's
development, you keep a record of my struggles. You
not only see my tears, but you also *save* them. I can
only conclude that I am precious to you, both in my
victories and in my struggles. As I go through the
necessary challenges of growth, you know and you
care. Thank you for being with me.

Are not two sparrows sold for a penny? Yet not
one of them will fall to the ground apart from
your Father. And even the hairs of your head
are all counted. So do not be afraid; you
are of more value than many sparrows.

—Matthew 10:29–31

December 11

I will sing to the Lord as long as I live;
I will sing praise to my God while I have being.
May my meditation be pleasing to him,
for I rejoice in the Lord.

Psalm 104:33–34

Look upon us,
O Lord, and let
all the darkness of our souls
vanish before the beams of
thy brightness. Fill us with
holy love, and open to us the
treasures of thy wisdom. All our desire is known unto
thee, therefore perfect what thou hast begun, and
what thy Spirit has awakened us to ask in prayer.
We seek thy face, turn thy face unto us and show us
thy glory. Then shall our longing be satisfied, and
our peace shall be perfect.

—St. Augustine

[The angels] fell on their faces before the throne
and worshiped God, singing, "Amen! Blessing
and glory and wisdom and thanksgiving
and honor and power and might be to
our God forever and ever! Amen."

—Revelation 7:11–12

December 12

Praise the Lord!
Happy are those who fear the Lord,
who greatly delight in his commandments.

Psalm 112:1

Dear Lord, I'm grappling with these two reactions of "fear" and "delight." This psalm seems to put them together as if they're synonyms, but they seem completely opposite. I delight in friends and loved ones. I fear terrorists and the IRS. Can I delight in you while still being afraid of you? How is that supposed to work? Maybe "fear" is mainly a recognition that you pay attention to what I do. The way I live my life matters to you. Then "delight" could be the knowledge that you help me live right and that you forgive me when I don't. Teach me more, O Lord, about this mixture of emotions.

For you did not receive a spirit of slavery to fall back into fear, but you have received a spirit of adoption. When we cry, "Abba! Father!" it is that very Spirit bearing witness with our spirit that we are children of God.

—Romans 8:15–16

December 13

The Lord sets the prisoners free;
the Lord opens the eyes of the blind.
The Lord lifts up those who are bowed down;
the Lord loves the righteous.

Psalm 146:7–8

Consumed by frustration,
    boxed in at every angle,
Unable to do what's necessary to
    get ahead,
Locked in bad relationships, caged
    by addictions,
I turn to you.
You set prisoners free.
Uncertain where to go next,
    learning little from the past,
Gazing at a hazy future and glimpsing nothing,
Looking past the people who love me,
Extremely near-sighted, I see only myself,
But then I turn to you.
You open the eyes of the blind.
Thank you, Lord.

Blessed are the poor in spirit, for theirs
is the kingdom of heaven.

—Matthew 5:3

December 14

You have multiplied, O Lord my God,
your wondrous deeds and your thoughts toward us;
none can compare with you.

Psalm 40:5

I start adding up your blessings to me, dear Lord, and I need a calculator. In fact, your goodness to me multiplies blessings times blessings. I thank you for every one of them. Every smile from someone I love. Every word we exchange. Every breath I draw and every beat of my heart. Every color in the spectrum of an evening sky or a bird's plumage. The taste of my favorite food. The wetness of water on a sweltering day. I thank you for all these things and more.

"For who has known the mind of the Lord? Or who has been his counselor?" "Or who has given a gift to him, to receive a gift in return?" For from him and through him and to him are all things. To him be the glory forever. Amen.

—Romans 11:34–36

December 15

I will thank you forever,
because of what you have done.
In the presence of the faithful
I will proclaim your name, for it is good.

Psalm 52:9

Now thank we all our God with heart
and hand and voices,
Who wondrous things has done, in whom this
world rejoices;
Who from our mothers' arms has blessed us on our way
With countless gifts of love, and still is ours today.
O may this bounteous God through all our life be
near us,
With ever-joyful hearts and blessed peace to cheer us;
And keeps us still in grace, and guides us when
perplexed;
And frees us from all ills in this world and the next.
All praise and thanks to God the Father now be given;
The Son and him who reigns with them in highest
heaven;
The one eternal God, whom earth and heaven adore;
For thus it was, is now, and shall be evermore.

Praise the Lord with shouts of everlasting joy.

December 16

Who can utter the mighty doings of the Lord,
or declare all his praise?

Psalm 106:2

My beautiful Lord, there are not enough words in my vocabulary to praise you as you deserve. The dictionary itself doesn't contain enough words. If I knew every language on Earth, there would still be inadequate words to say how great you really are. Simple phrases like "awesome God" and "wonderful Savior" seem entirely too easy, but I'll use those, and I'll make up other praises. Yet, even more than that, I will *live out* my praises, putting my love for you into action. I will seek, today and every day, to live in a way that brings pleasure to you. Dear Lord, I love you.

Let us continually offer a sacrifice of praise to God, that is, the fruit of lips that confess his name. Do not neglect to do good and to share what you have, for such sacrifices are pleasing to God.

—Hebrews 13:15–16

December 17

Let me hear of your steadfast love in the morning,
for in you I put my trust.
Teach me the way I should go,
for to you I lift up my soul.

Psalm 143:8

ord, thou hast given us thy Word for a light to shine upon our path; grant us so to meditate on that Word, and to follow its teaching, that we may find in it the light that shines more and more until the perfect day; through Jesus Christ our Lord.

—Saint Jerome

The Lord will guide you continually,
and satisfy your needs in parched places,
and make your bones strong;
and you shall be like a watered garden,
like a spring of water,
whose waters never fail.

—Isaiah 58:11

December 18

Wash me thoroughly from my iniquity,
and cleanse me from my sin.

Psalm 51:2

O Lord, who hast mercy upon all, take away
from me my sins, and mercifully kindle
in me the fire of thy Holy Spirit. Take away from me
the heart of stone, and give me a heart of flesh,
a heart to love and adore thee,
a heart to delight in thee,
to follow and to enjoy thee,
for Christ's sake.

—Ambrose of Milan

He chose us in Christ...to be holy and
blameless before him in love.... In him
we have redemption through his blood,
the forgiveness of our trespasses,
according to the riches of his
grace that he lavished on us.

—Ephesians 1:4, 7–8

December 19

Bless the Lord, O you his angels,
you mighty ones who do his bidding,
obedient to his spoken word.
Bless the Lord, all his hosts,
his ministers that do his will.

Psalm 103:20–21

At this time of year, almighty Father, I think of the angels who put this psalm into practice one night in the skies over Bethlehem. They truly blessed you, Lord, singing, "Glory to God in the highest." What an amazing sight that must have been! And how I'd love to hear the sounds of that celestial choir! Maybe someday, when we're all in heaven together, I'll ask them for a repeat performance. Lord, I thank you for the ministry of those angels, who delivered to humanity the most important message ever.

Then an angel of the Lord stood before them, and the glory of the Lord shone around them, and they were terrified. But the angel said to them, "Do not be afraid."

—Luke 2:9–10

December 20

The Lord says to my lord,
"Sit at my right hand
until I make your enemies your footstool."
The Lord sends out from Zion
your mighty scepter.

Psalm 110:1–2

A new king was born in Bethlehem, laid in a manger, announced by angels, and worshipped by wise men. Lord God, you handed authority to the Lord Jesus in order to accomplish a daring rescue mission. It's amazing, when I think about it, that you were venturing into enemy territory. Earth was, and is, full of people who resent you, resist you, and reject you— and still you entrusted the royal child to this hurting planet. It's a magnificent story, and it makes me want to worship you even more. Amen.

Jesus used this psalm to explain his unique identity as both God and man, since the Lord God was granting authority to someone even King David (the psalmist) called "my lord."

372

December 21

Make a joyful noise to the Lord, all the earth; . . .
Let the floods clap their hands;
let the hills sing together for joy
at the presence of the Lord, for he is coming
to judge the earth.

Psalm 98:4, 8–9

$\mathcal{L}$et me add my voice to the praisefest. If the seas and mountains can clap and sing, why shouldn't I? Along with all creation, I rejoice in your arrival, my Lord. Some might bristle at the thought of you "judging" the earth, but I know that means "setting things right." You came to our world to redeem us, to vanquish sin and death, and to restore us with the Creator. And so our response is truly joyful. This is good news, and it inspires an exultant song, today, this Christmas season, as well as all year round.

The Christmas carol "Joy to the World" was based on Psalm 98. You might recall "fields and floods, rocks, hills, and plains" from the second verse.

December 22

Yet God my King is from of old,
working salvation in the earth.

Psalm 74:12

Hail the heaven-born Prince of Peace!
   Hail the Sun of Righteousness!
Light and life to all he brings,
Risen with healing in his wings,
Mild he lays his glory by,
Born that we no more may die,
Born to raise us from the earth,
Born to give us second birth.
Hark the herald angels sing,
"Glory to the newborn king!"

—Charles Wesley

"I am bringing you good news of great joy for
all the people: to you is born this day in the city
of David a Savior, who is the Messiah, the Lord."

—Luke 2:10–11

December 23

Make vows to the Lord your God, and perform them;
let all who are around him bring gifts
to the one who is awesome.

Psalm 76:11

What gifts do I have to bring to you, most awesome Lord? Gold? Well, my accounts are limited. Frankincense and myrrh? I'm not sure how to get those things or how to give

them. But I think you want more from me anyway. My attention? My creativity? The risks I take to love others? As people rush out to buy last-minute presents to put under the tree, I want to give you something truly special. Tell me, Lord: What do you want for Christmas?

On entering the house, they saw the child with Mary his mother; and they knelt down and paid him homage. Then, opening their treasure chests, they offered him gifts of gold, frankincense, and myrrh.

—Matthew 2:11

December 24

ngels, from the realms of glory, wing
   your flight over all the earth.
Ye who sang creation's story, now proclaim Messiah's
   birth.
Come and worship, come and worship. Worship
   Christ, the newborn king.
Shepherds, in the field abiding, watching over your
   flocks by night,
God with man is now residing. Yonder shines the
   infant light.
Come and worship, come and worship. Worship
   Christ, the newborn king.

—James Montgomery

When they saw this, they made known what
   had been told them about this child;
   and all who heard it were amazed
   at what the shepherds told them.

—Luke 2:17–18

December 25

I will tell of the decree of the Lord:
He said to me, "You are my son;
today I have begotten you."

Psalm 2:7

Today we celebrate the birth of your only begotten Son, our Lord and Savior, Jesus Christ. The mystery of Christmas is deep and compelling—how and even why your Son was born a baby. For him to pour himself into human flesh, to become a baby, and to consent to be born in a stable—this is beyond our comprehension. It was an act of supreme love, and I praise you for it. When all the presents have been opened, when the feast is cleared away, when the shreds of wrapping paper are discarded, and when the sparkling lights turned off, this will stay with me—the remarkable love of the one who made me.

What wondrous love is this
That caused the Lord of bliss
To bear the dreadful curse
For my soul?

—Folk Hymn

December 26

God, your God, has anointed you
with the oil of gladness beyond your companions;
your robes are all fragrant with myrrh and aloes and cassia.
From ivory palaces stringed instruments make you glad.

Psalm 45:7–8

Today's psalm paints a royal portrait—a king enjoying palace life. I wonder if this is a glimpse of your heavenly life, before you came to earth to be born. If so, it's a stark contrast to the stable. Fragrant robes replaced with swaddling clothes. Suddenly your "companions" are oxen and donkeys. This is what you gave up in order to save us. I love the fact that one of these royal scents is myrrh. The magi knew you were a king, and they offered a whiff of majesty. Lord Jesus, thank you for becoming one of us. In your precious name, I pray. Amen.

Christ Jesus...though he was in the form of God, did not regard equality with God as something to be exploited, but emptied himself, taking the form of a slave, being born in human likeness.

—Philippians 2:5–7

December 27

By awesome deeds you answer us with deliverance,
O God of our salvation;
you are the hope of all the ends of the earth
and of the farthest seas.

Psalm 65:5

O God of our salvation, your most awesome deed was the sending of your Son. His incarnation as a human being restored the worth of your creation. His sacrifice for our sin won our freedom. His resurrection from the

grave established your power over death. And we are the beneficiaries. Thank you, Lord, for this greatest of all gifts. I know I can never repay you, but I offer you a song in my heart, a prayer in my soul, and the love that drives me forward each day. Blessings to you, unfathomable God.

Thanks be to God for his indescribable gift!

—2 Corinthians 9:15

December 28

Then we your people, the flock of your pasture,
will give thanks to you forever;
from generation to generation we will recount your praise.

Psalm 79:13

Dear Lord, as each year draws to a close, I begin to take a long look at myself. Where is my life headed? What am I accomplishing? And what will I leave behind when my time on Earth is up? I'm grateful for the way you've worked in my life, but now I look to the next generation. Have I passed on any faith or wisdom to the younger set? Have I mentored anyone to take my place—whatever

that place might be? Have I inspired the next generation to praise you? Lord, let this be the focus of the coming year for me. Let me pass forward your praises.

You then, my child, be strong in the grace that is in Christ Jesus; and what you have heard from me through many witnesses entrust to faithful people who will be able to teach others as well.

—2 Timothy 2:1–2

December 29

Will you not revive us again,
so that your people may rejoice in you?

Psalm 85:6

The week between Christmas and New Year's Day is always an interesting time, dear Lord. Sure, the malls are packed with people returning gifts they don't want, but there's a spiritual character to these days as well. We just finished celebrating the wonder of incarnation: "God becoming human." So now what? Has this awesome story changed us in any way? And now that we're looking forward to a new year, in which the slate gets wiped clean, can we start afresh? In this in-between time I look to you for guidance. How will the blessings of Christmas take hold in my life? And how will I live out the truth of Christmas in the coming year?

You've heard, "Keep Christ in Christmas."
Maybe we should also say, "Keep
Christmas in Christians."

December 30

For a thousand years in your sight
are like yesterday when it is past,
or like a watch in the night.

Psalm 90:4

*W*ell, that was fast. Seems as if just yesterday I was compiling resolutions for this past year—all the self-improvements I was determined to make. How far did I get with those? February? June? September? Time flies. And if that's true for me, what must it be like for you? A millennium is a day. Lord, I want your perspective on life. I want to take the large view. I fret so much about momentary things, but if I get the big picture will I see what's really important? Let me invest my life in things that matter—relationships, worship, using the gifts you've given me to return glory to you. Life is too short to trudge along in daily dread. I want to connect each day to eternity.

Do not worry about tomorrow, for tomorrow will bring worries of its own. Today's trouble is enough for today.

—Matthew 6:34

December 31

Surely goodness and mercy shall follow me
all the days of my life,
and I shall dwell in the house of the Lord
my whole life long.

Psalm 23:6

My loving Lord, I thank you for the past year with all its joys and struggles. There were delightful moments of love shared with special people. I bask in those memories. Yet there were also challenges—heartaches, losses, and disappointments. As I look back, I recognize that you stayed with me in those tough times. I came to know you in a whole new way. Thank you, Lord, for your care and guidance, step by step, day by day. Your goodness and mercy have indeed followed me. I've been blessed. In Jesus' wondrous name, I pray. Amen.

Eternity isn't just some future promise of a timeless existence. It's a *quality* of life, lived in the embrace of an everlasting God. For the believer, eternal life has already begun. Praise the Lord!

ACKNOWLEDGMENTS:

Publications International, Ltd., has made every effort to locate the owners of all copyrighted material to obtain permission to use the selections that appear in this book. Any errors or omissions are unintentional; corrections, if necessary, will be made in future editions.

Pages 15, 205: Taken from *My Utmost for His Highest* by Oswald Chambers, edited by James Reimann, © 1992 by Oswald Chambers Publications Assn., Ltd., and used by permission of Discovery House Publishers, Grand Rapids MI 49501. All rights reserved.

Page 70: Reprinted with permission of Christine A. Dallman. Copyright © 2000.

Pages 77, 195, 281, 346: Taken from *Faith Alone: A Daily Devotional,* selections taken from works of Martin Luther, edited by James C. Galvin. Copyright © 1998 by Zondervan. Used by permission of Zondervan. www.zondervan.com

Pages 82, 136, 162, 350: Taken from the book *The World According to Mister Rogers: Important Things to Remember* by Fred Rogers. Copyright © 2003 Family Communications, Inc. Reprinted by permission of Hyperion. All rights reserved

Page 211: Taken from *The Pursuit of God* by A. W. Tozer. Copyright © 1982 by Wing Spread Publishers, Camp Hill, PA. Used by permission of Wing Spread Publishers.

Page 279: Reprinted with the permission of Scribner, a Division of Simon & Schuster, Inc., from *A Diary of Private Prayer* by John Baillie. Copyright © 1949 by Charles Scribner's Sons; copyright renewed © 1977 by Ian Fowler Baillie. All rights reserved.

Unless otherwise noted, all Scripture quotations are taken from the *New Revised Standard Version* of the Bible. Copyright © 1989 by the Division of Christian Education of the National Council of the Churches of Christ in the United States of America. Used by permission. All rights reserved.

Scripture quotations marked (KJV) are taken from *The Holy Bible, King James Version.* Copyright © 1977, 1984, Thomas Nelson Inc., Publishers.

Scripture quotations marked (NASB) are taken from *The Holy Bible, New American Standard Bible.* Copyright © 1977, Holman Bible Publishers. Used by Permission. All rights reserved.

Scripture quotations marked (NIV) are taken from *The Holy Bible, New International Version.* Copyright © 1973, 1978, 1984, International Bible Society. Used by permission of Zondervan Publishing House. All rights reserved.

Scripture quotations marked (NKJV) are taken from the *New King James Version.* Copyright © 1979, 1980, 1982 by Thomas Nelson, Inc. Used by permission. All rights reserved.

Scripture quotations marked (NLT) are taken from the *Holy Bible, New Living Translation.* Copyright © 1996. Used by permission of Tyndale House Publishers, Inc., Wheaton, IL 60187. All rights reserved.

Scripture quotations marked (RSV) are taken from the *Revised Standard Version of the Bible.* Copyright © 1952, by the Division of Christian Education of the National Council of the Churches of Christ in the U.S.A. Used by permission. All rights reserved.

Scripture quotations marked (TLB) are taken from *The Living Bible.* Copyright © 1971. Used by permission of Tyndale House Publishers, Inc. All rights reserved.